Faith and Prejudice

FAITH AND PREJUDICE

CATHOLIC SERMONS

OF

BL. JOHN HENRY NEWMAN

ASSUMPTION
PRESS

2013

The Parting of Friends was originally published in *Sermons on Subjects of the Day*, by Longmans, Green, and Co. in 1902. *Faith and Prejudice* was first published by Sheed and Ward in 1956.

Cover image: *John Henry Newman*, John Everett Millais, 1881

Contents

Faith
and
Prejudice

THE PARTING OF FRIENDS

*Preached on the anniversary of
the consecration of a chapel
25th September, 1843*

"MAN GOETH FORTH TO HIS WORK AND TO
HIS LABOUR UNTIL THE EVENING." (PS 104:23).

When the Son of Man, the First-born of the creation of God, came to the evening of His mortal life, He parted with His disciples at a feast. He had borne "the burden and heat of the day;" yet, when "wearied with His journey," He had but stopped at the well's side, and asked a draught of water for His thirst; for He had "meat to eat which" others "knew not of." His meat was "to do the will of Him that sent Him, and to finish His work;" "I must work the works of Him that sent Me," said He, "while it is day; the night cometh, when no man can work" (John 4:6, 34; 9:4). Thus passed the season of His ministry; and if at any time He feasted with Pharisee or publican, it was in order that He might do the work of God more strenuously. But "when the even was come He sat down with the Twelve." "And He said unto them, With desire have I desired to eat this Passover with you, before I suffer" (Matt 26: 20). He was about to suffer more than man had ever suffered or shall suffer. But there is nothing gloomy, churlish, violent, or selfish in His grief; it is tender, affectionate, social. He calls His friends around Him, though He was as Job among the ashes; He bids them stay by Him, and see Him suffer; He desires their sympathy; He takes refuge in their love. He first feasted them, and sung a hymn with them, and washed their feet; and when His long trial began, He beheld them and kept them in His presence, till they in terror shrank from it. Yet, on St. Mary and St. John, His Virgin Mother and His Virgin Disciple, who remained, His eyes still rested; and in St. Peter, who was denying Him in the distance, His sudden glance wrought a deep repentance. O wonderful pattern, the type of all trial and of all duty under it, while the Church endures.

We indeed today have no need of so high a lesson and so august a comfort. We have no pain, no grief which calls for it; yet, considering it has been brought before us in this morning's service, we are naturally drawn to think of it, though it be infinitely above us, under certain circumstances of this season and the present time. For now are the shades of evening falling upon the earth, and the year's labour is coming to its end. In Septuagesima the labourers were sent into the vineyard; in Sexagesima the sower went forth to sow;—that time is over; "the harvest is passed, the summer is ended" (Jer 8:20), the vintage is gathered. We have kept the Ember-days for the fruits of the earth, in self-abasement, as being unworthy even of the least of God's mercies; and now we are offering up of its corn and wine as a propitiation, and are eating and drinking of them with thanksgiving.

"All things come of Thee, and of Thine own have we given Thee" (1 Chr. 29:14). If we have had the rain in its season, and the sun shining in its strength, and the fertile ground, it is of Thee. We give back to Thee what came from Thee. "When Thou givest it them, they gather it, and when Thou openest Thy hand, they are filled with good. When Thou hidest Thy face, they are troubled; when Thou takest away their breath, they die, and are turned again to their dust. When Thou lettest Thy breath go forth, they shall be made, and Thou shalt renew the face of the earth" (Ps 104:28-30). He gives, He takes away. "Shall we receive good at the hand of God, and shall we not receive evil?" (Job 2:10) May He not "do what He will with His own?" (Matt 20:15) May not His sun set as it has risen? and must it not set, if it is to rise again? and must not darkness come first, if there is ever to be morning? and must not the sky be blacker, before it can be brighter? And cannot He, who can do all things, cause a light to arise even in the darkness? "I have thought upon Thy Name,

O Lord, in the night season, and have kept Thy Law;" "Thou also shalt light my candle, the Lord my God shall make my darkness to be light;" or as the Prophet speaks, "At the evening time it shall be light" (Zech 14:7).

"All things come of Thee," says holy David, "for we are strangers before Thee and sojourners, as were all our fathers; our days on the earth are as a shadow, and there is none abiding" (1 Chr 29:15). All is vanity, vanity of vanities, and vexation of spirit. "What profit hath a man of all his labour which he taketh under the sun? One generation passeth away, and another generation cometh; but the earth abideth for ever; the sun also ariseth, and the sun goeth down; ... all things are full of labour, man cannot utter it; ... that which is crooked cannot be made straight, and that which is wanting cannot be numbered" (Eccl 1:3-15). "To every thing there is a season, and a time to every purpose under heaven; a time to be born and a time to die; a time to plant and a time to pluck up that which is planted; a time to kill and a time to heal; a time to break down and a time to build up; ... a time to get and a time to lose; a time to keep and a time to cast away." (Eccl 3:1-6). And time, and matter, and motion, and force, and the will of man, how vain are they all, except as instruments of the grace of God, blessing them and working with them! How vain are all our pains, our thought, our care, unless God uses them, unless God has inspired them! how worse than fruitless are they, unless directed to His glory, and given back to the Giver!

"Of Thine own have we given Thee," says the royal Psalmist, after he had collected materials for the Temple. Because "the work was great," and "the palace, not for man, but for the Lord God," therefore he "prepared with all his might for the house of his God," gold, and silver, and brass, and iron, and wood, "onyx stones, and stones to be set, glistering stones, and of divers colours, and all manner of precious stones, and marble stones in abundance" (1 Chr 29:1, 2, 9). And "the people rejoiced, for that they offered willingly; ... and David the king also rejoiced with great joy." We too, at this season, year by year, have been allowed in our measure, according to our work and our faith, to rejoice in God's Presence, for this sacred building which He has given us to worship Him in. It was a glad time when we first met here,—many of us now present recollect it; nor did our rejoicing cease, but was renewed every autumn, as the day came round. It has been "a day of gladness and feasting, and a good day, and of sending portions one to another" (Esth 9:19). We have kept the feast heretofore with merry hearts; we have kept it seven full years unto "a perfect end;" now let us keep it, even though in haste, and with bitter herbs, and with loins girded, and with a staff in our hand, as they who have "no continuing city, but seek one to come" (Heb 8:14).

So was it with Jacob, when with his staff he passed over that Jordan. He too kept feast before he set out upon his dreary way. He received a father's blessing, and then was sent afar; he left his mother, never to see her face or hear her voice again. He parted with all that his heart loved, and turned his face towards a strange land. He went with the doubt, whether he should have bread to eat, or raiment to put on. He came to "the people of the East," and served a hard master twenty years. "In the day the drought consumed him, and the frost by night; and his sleep departed from his eyes" (Gen 31:40). O little did he think, when father and mother had forsaken him, and at Bethel he lay down to sleep on the desolate ground, because the sun was set and even had come, that there was the house of God and the gate of heaven, that the Lord was in that place, and would thence go forward with him whithersoever he went, till He brought him back to that river in "two bands," who was then crossing it forlorn and solitary!

So had it been with Ishmael; though the feast was not to him a blessing, yet he feasted in his father's tent, and then was sent away. That tender father, who, when a son was promised him of Sarah, cried out to his Almighty Protector, "O that Ishmael might live before Thee!" (Gen 17:18)—he it was, who, under a divine direction, the day after the feast, "rose up early in the morning, and took bread, and a bottle of water, and gave it unto Hagar, putting it on her shoulder, and the child, and sent her away. And she departed, and wandered in the wilderness of Beersheba" (Gen 21:14). And little thought that fierce child, when for feasting came thirst and weariness and wandering in the desert, that this was not the end of Ishmael, but the beginning. And little did Hagar read his coming fortunes, when "the water was spent in the bottle, and she cast the child under one of the shrubs, and she went and sat her down over against him a good way off; ... for she said, Let me not see the death of the child. And she sat over against him, and lift up her voice, and wept."

So had it been with Naomi, though she was not quitting, but returning to her home, and going, not to a land of famine, but of plenty. In a time of distress, she had left her country, and found friends and made relatives among the enemies of her people. And when her husband and her children died, Moabitish women, who had once been the stumbling-block of Israel, became the support and comfort of her widowhood. Time had been when, at the call of the daughters of Moab, the chosen people had partaken their sacrifices, and "bowed down to their gods. And Israel joined himself unto Baal-peor, and the anger of the Lord was kindled against Israel." Centuries had since passed away, and now of Moabites was Naomi mother; and to their land had she given her heart, when the call of duty summoned her back to Bethlehem. "She had heard in the country of Moab, how that the Lord had visited His people in giving them bread. Wherefore she went forth out of the place where she was, and her two daughters-in-law with her, and they went on the way to return unto the land of Judah" (Ruth 1:6-8, 14, 15).

Forlorn widow, great was the struggle in her bosom, whether shall she do?—leave behind her the two heathen women, in widowhood and weakness like herself, her sole stay, the shadows of departed blessings? or shall she selfishly take them as fellow-sufferers, who could not be protectors? Shall she seek sympathy where she cannot gain help? shall she deprive them of a home, when she has none to supply? So she said, "Go, return each to her mother's house: the Lord deal kindly with you, as ye have dealt with the dead and with me!" Perplexed Naomi, torn with contrary feelings; which tried her the more,—Orpah who left her, or Ruth who remained? Orpah who was a pain, or Ruth who was a charge? "They lifted up their voice and wept again; and Orpah kissed her mother-in-law, but Ruth clave unto her. And she said, Behold, thy sister-in-law is gone back unto her people and unto her gods; return thou after thy sister-in-law. And Ruth said, Entreat me not to leave thee, or to return from following after thee: for whither thou goest, I will go; and where thou lodgest, I will lodge: thy people shall be my people, and thy God my God. Where thou diest, will I die, and there will I be buried; the Lord do so to me, and more also, if aught but death part thee and me" (Ruth 1:14-17).

Orpah kissed Naomi, and went back to the world. There was sorrow in the parting, but Naomi's sorrow was more for Orpah's sake than for her own. Pain there would be, but it was the pain of a wound, not the yearning regret of love. It was the pain we feel when friends disappoint us, and fall in our esteem. That kiss of Orpah was no loving token; it was but the hollow profession of those who use smooth words, that they may part company with us with least trouble and discomfort to themselves. Orpah's tears were but the dregs of affection; she clasped her mother-in-law once for all, that she might not cleave to her. Far different were the tears, far different the embrace, which passed between those two religious friends recorded in the book which follows, who loved each other with a true love unfeigned, but whose lives ran in different courses. If Naomi's grief was great when Orpah kissed her, what was David's when he saw the last of him, whose "soul had from the first been knit with his soul," so that "he loved him as his own soul"? (1 Sam 18:1-3). "I am distressed for thee, my brother Jonathan," he says; "very pleasant hast thou been unto me; thy love to me was wonderful, passing the love of women" (2 Sam 1:26). What woe was upon that "young man," "of a beautiful countenance and goodly to look to," and "cunning in playing, and a mighty valiant man, and a man of war, and prudent in matters;" (1 Sam 16:12, 18). when his devoted affectionate loyal friend, whom these good gifts have gained, looked upon him for the last time! O hard destiny, except that the All-merciful so willed it, that such companions might not walk in the house of God as friends! David must flee to the wilderness, Jonathan must pine in his father's hall; Jonathan must share that stern father's death in battle, and David must ascend the vacant throne. Yet they made a covenant on parting: "Thou shalt not only," said Jonathan, "while yet I live, show me the kindness of the Lord, that I die not; but also thou shalt not cut off thy kindness from my house for ever; no, not when the Lord hath cut off the enemies of David, every one from the face of the earth ... And Jonathan caused David to swear again, because he loved him, for he loved him as he loved his own soul." And then, while David hid himself, Jonathan made trial of Saul, how he felt disposed to David; and when he found that "it was determined of his father to slay David," he "arose from the table in fierce anger, and did eat no meat the second day of the mouth; for he was grieved for David, because his father had done him shame." Then in the morning he went out into the field, where David lay, and the last meeting took place between the two. "David arose out of a place toward the south, and fell on his face to the ground, and bowed himself three times; and they kissed one another, and wept one with another, till David exceeded. And Jonathan said to David, Go in peace, forasmuch as we have sworn both of us in the Name of the Lord, saying, The Lord be between me and thee, and between my seed and thy seed for ever. And he arose and departed; and Jonathan went into the city" (1 Sam 20:14-42).

David's affection was given to a single heart; but there is another spoken of in Scripture, who had a thousand friends and loved each as his own soul, and seemed to live a thousand lives in them, and died a thousand deaths when he must quit them: that great Apostle, whose very heart was broken when his brethren wept; who "lived if they stood fast in the Lord;" who "was glad when he was weak and they were strong;" and who was "willing to have imparted unto them his own soul, because they were dear unto him" (Acts 21:21, 22; 1 Thess 2:8; 3:8; 2 Cor 8:9). Yet we read of his bidding farewell to whole Churches, never to see them again. At one time, to the little ones of the flock; "When we had accomplished those days," says the Evangelist, "we departed, and went our way, ... with wives and children, till we were out of the city; and we kneeled down on the shore and prayed. And when we had taken our leave one of another, we took ship, and they returned home again." At another time, to the rulers of the Church: "And now behold," he says to them, "I know that ye all,

11

among whom I have gone preaching the kingdom of God, shall see my face no more. Wherefore, I take you to record this day, that I am pure from the blood of all men, for I have not shunned to declare unto you all the counsel of God ... I have coveted no man's silver, or gold, or apparel; ... I have showed you all things, how that so labouring he ought to support the weak; and to remember the words of the Lord Jesus, how he said, It is more blessed to give than to receive." And then, when he had finished, "he kneeled down, and prayed with them all. And they all wept sore, and fell on Paul's neck, and kissed him; sorrowing most of all for the words which he spake, that they should see his face no more. And they accompanied him unto the ship" (Acts 21:5, 6; 20:25-27, 33, 35, 36-38).

There was another time, when he took leave of his "own son in the faith," Timothy, in words more calm, and still more impressive, when his end was nigh: "I am now ready to be offered," he says, "and the time of my departure is at hand. I have fought a good fight, I have finished my course, I have kept the faith. Henceforth there is laid up for me a crown of righteousness, which the Lord, the Righteous Judge, shall give me at that day" (2 Tim 4:6-8).

And what are all these instances but memorials and tokens of the Son of Man, when His work and His labour were coming to an end? Like Jacob, like Ishmael, like Elisha, like the Evangelist whose day is just passed, He kept feast before His departure; and, like David, He was persecuted by the rulers in Israel; and, like Naomi, He was deserted by His friends; and, like Ishmael, He cried out, "I thirst" in a barren and dry land; and at length, like Jacob, He went to sleep with a stone for His pillow, in the evening. And, like St. Paul, He had "finished the work which God gave Him to do," and had "witnessed a good confession" (1 Tim 6:13); and, beyond St. Paul, "the Prince of this world had come, and had nothing in Him" (John 14:30). "He was in the world, and the world was made by Him, and the world knew Him not. He came unto His own, and His own received Him not" (John 1:10, 11). Heavily did He leave, tenderly did He mourn over the country and city which rejected Him. "When He was come near, He beheld the city, and wept over it, saying, If thou hadst known, even thou, at least in this thy day, the things which belong unto thy peace! but now they are hid from thine eyes." And again: "O Jerusalem, Jerusalem, which killest the prophets, and stonest them that are sent unto thee, how often would I have gathered thy children together, as a hen doth gather her brood under her wings, and ye would not! Behold, your house is left unto you desolate" (Luke 19:41, 42; 13:34, 35).

A lesson surely, and a warning to us all, in every place where He puts His Name, to the end of time; lest we be cold towards His gifts, or unbelieving towards His word, or jealous of His workings, or heartless towards His mercies ... O mother of saints! O school of the wise! O nurse of the heroic! of whom went forth, in whom have dwelt, memorable names of old, to spread the truth abroad, or to cherish and illustrate it at home! O thou, from whom surrounding nations lit their lamps! O virgin of Israel! wherefore dost thou now sit on the ground and keep silence, like one of the foolish women who were without oil on the coming of the Bridegroom? Where is now the ruler in Sion, and the doctor in the Temple, and the ascetic on Carmel, and the herald in the wilderness, and the preacher in the market-place? where are thy "effectual fervent prayers," offered in secret, and thy alms and good works coming up as a memorial before God? How is it, O once holy place, that "the land mourneth, for the corn is wasted, the new wine is dried up, the oil languisheth, ... because joy is withered away from the sons of men?" "Alas for the day! ... how do the beasts groan! the herds of cattle are perplexed, because they have no pasture, yea, the flocks of sheep are made desolate" (Joel 1:10-18). "Lebanon is ashamed and hewn down; Sharon is like a wilderness, and Bashan and Carmel shake off their fruits" (Isa 23:9). O my mother, whence is this unto thee, that thou hast good things poured upon thee and canst not keep them, and bearest children, yet darest not own them? why hast thou not the skill to use their services, nor the heart to rejoice in their love? how is it that whatever is generous in purpose, and tender or deep in devotion, thy flower and thy promise, falls from thy bosom and finds no home within thine arms? Who hath put this note upon thee, to have "a miscarrying womb, and dry breasts," to be strange to thine own flesh, and thine eye cruel towards thy little ones? Thine own offspring, the fruit of thy womb, who love thee and would toil for thee, thou dost gaze upon with fear, as though a portent, or thou dost loathe as an offence;—at best thou dost but endure, as if they had no claim but on thy patience, self-possession, and vigilance, to be rid of them as easily as thou mayest. Thou makest them "stand all the day idle," as the very condition of thy bearing with them; or thou biddest them be gone, where they will be more welcome; or thou sellest them for nought to the stranger that passes by. And what wilt thou do in the end thereof? ...

Scripture is a refuge in any trouble; only let us be on our guard against seeming to use it further than is fitting, or doing more than sheltering ourselves under its shadow. Let us use it according to our measure. It is far higher and wider than our need; and its language veils our feelings while it gives expression to them. It is sacred and heavenly; and it restrains and purifies, while it sanctions them.

And now, my brethren, "bless God, praise Him and magnify Him, and praise Him for the things which He hath done unto you in the sight of all that live. It is good to praise God, and exalt His Name, and honourably to show forth the works of God; therefore be not slack to praise Him" (Tob 12:6). "All the works of the Lord are good; and He will give every needful thing in due season; so that a man cannot say, This is worse than that; for in time they shall all be well approved. And therefore praise ye the Lord with the whole heart and mouth, and bless the Name of the Lord" (Eccl 39:33-35).

"Leave off from wrath, and let go displeasure; flee from evil, and do the thing that is good" (Ps 37:8, 27). "Do that which is good, and no evil shall touch you" (Tob 12:7). "Go your way; eat your bread with joy, and drink your wine with a merry heart, for God now accepteth your works; let your garments be always white, and let your head lack no ointment" (Eccl 9:7, 8).

And, O my brethren, O kind and affectionate hearts, O loving friends, should you know any one whose lot it has been, by writing or by word of mouth, in some degree to help you thus to act; if he has ever told you what you knew about yourselves, or what you did not know; has read to you your wants or feelings, and comforted you by the very reading; has made you feel that there was a higher life than this daily one, and a brighter world than that you see; or encouraged you, or sobered you, or opened a way to the inquiring, or soothed the perplexed; if what he has said or done has ever made you take interest in him, and feel well inclined towards him; remember such a one in time to come, though you hear him not, and pray for him, that in all things he may know God's will, and at all times he may be ready to fulfil it.

THE OMNIPOTENCE OF GOD THE REASON FOR FAITH AND HOPE

Fourth Sunday after Epiphany,
30th January 1848

OUR LORD commanded the winds and the sea, and the men who saw it marvelled saying, What manner of man is this, for the winds and the sea obey him? It was a miracle. It showed our Lord's power over nature. And therefore they wondered, because they could not understand, and rightly, how any man could have power over nature, unless that power was given him by God. Nature goes on her own way and we cannot alter it. Man cannot alter it, he can only use it. Matter, for instance, falls downward, earth, stone, iron all fall to the earth when left to themselves. Again, left to themselves, they cannot move *except* by falling. They never move except they are pulled or pushed forward. Water again never stands in a heap or a mass, but flows out on all sides as far as it can. Fire again always burns, or tends to burn. The wind blows to and fro, without any discoverable rule or law, and we cannot tell how it will blow tomorrow by seeing how it blows today. We see all these things. They have their own way; we cannot alter them. All we attempt to do is to use them; we take them as we find them and we use them. We don't attempt to change the nature of fire, earth, air or water, but we observe what the nature of each is, and we try to turn it to account. We turn steam to account, and use it in carriages and ships; we turn fire to account and use it in a thousand ways. We use the things of nature, we submit to the laws of nature, and we avail ourselves of them; but we do not command nature. We do not attempt to alter it, but we merely direct it to our own purposes. Far different was it with our Lord: He used indeed the winds and the water; (He used the water when He got into a boat, and used the wind when He suffered the sail to be spread over Him). He used, but more than this, He commanded, the winds and the waves—He had power to rebuke, to change, to undo the course of nature, as well as to make use of it. He was above nature. He had power over nature. This is what made the men marvel. Experienced seamen can make use of the winds and the waves to get to the shore. Nay, even in a storm they know how to avail themselves of them, they have their rules what to do, and they are on the look out, taking advantage of everything that happens. But our Lord did not condescend to do this. He did not instruct them how to manage their sails, nor how to steer the vessel, but He addressed Himself directly to winds and waves, and stopped them, making them do that which was against their nature.

So again, when Lazarus was ill, our Lord might have gone to him, and have recommended the fitting medicine, and the treatment which would cure him. He did nothing of the kind—He let him die—so much so that St. Martha said when He at length came, "Lord, if Thou hadst been here, my brother had not died" (John 11:21). But our Lord had a reason. He wished to show His power over nature. He wished to triumph over death. So, instead of hindering Lazarus from dying by the art of medicine, He triumphed over death by a miracle.

No one has power over nature but He who made it. None can work a miracle but God. When miracles are wrought it is a proof that God is present. And therefore it is that, whenever God visits the earth, He works miracles. It is the claim He makes upon our attention. He thereby reminds us that He is the Creator. He who did, alone can undo. He who made, alone can destroy. He who gave nature its laws, alone can change those laws. He who made fire to burn, food to nourish, water to flow, iron to sink, He alone can make fire harmless, food needless, water firm and solid, iron light, and therefore whether He sent forth the Prophets or the Apostles, Moses, Josue, Samuel,

21

or Elias, He always sent them with miracles, to show His presence with His servants. Then all things began to change their nature; the Egyptians were tormented with strange plagues, the waters stood in a heap for the Chosen people to pass over, they were fed with manna in the desert, the sun and the moon stood still—because God was there.

This then was what made the men marvel, when our Lord stilled the storm upon the sea. It was a proof to them that God was there, though they saw Him not. Nay, God was there and they saw Him—for Christ was God—but whether they learned this high and sacred truth or not from the miracle, so far they understood that God really was there. His hand was there, His power was there, and therefore they feared. You have read in books, I dare say, stories of great men who come in disguise, and at length are known by their voice, or by some deed, which betrays them. Their voices, or their words, or their manner, or their exploit, is their token—it is a sort of handwriting. And so when God walks the earth, He gives us means of knowing that He does so, though He is a hidden God, and does not display His glory openly. Power over nature is the token He gives us that He, the Creator of Nature, is in the midst of us.

And therefore God is called almighty—this is His distinguishing attribute. Man is powerful only by means of nature. He uses nature as his instrument, but God has no need of nature, in order to accomplish His will, but works His great work, sometimes by means of nature, and sometimes without nature, as it please Him.

And you will observe this attribute of God is the only one mentioned in the Creed. "I believe in God, the Father almighty." It is not said "I believe in God the Father All merciful, or All holy, or All wise," though all these attributes are His also, but "I believe in God the Father *Almighty*." Why is this? It is plain why—because this attribute is the reason *why* we *believe*. Faith is the beginning of religion, and therefore the almightiness of God is made the beginning and first of His attributes, and just the attribute which ought to be mentioned in the Creed. We should not be able to believe in Him, did we not know that He is almighty. Nothing is too hard to believe of Him to whom nothing is too hard to do. You may recollect that when it was prophesied to Abraham that the old Sarah his wife should have a son, Sarah laughed. Why did she laugh? Because she did not bear sufficiently in mind that God is almighty. Therefore the Lord said to her, "Is anything *hard* for God?" (Gen 18:14). And in like manner our Lord in the Gospel of this day, when He commanded the winds and the sea, said "Why are ye fearful, O ye of little *faith*?" If they had had a firm perception of His almightiness, they would have been sure that He could bring them out of danger. But when they saw Him asleep in the boat, they could not believe that they were safe, not understanding that He, awake or asleep, was almighty.

This thought is very important to us at this day, because it will be a means of sustaining our faith. Why do you believe all the strange and marvellous acts recorded in Scripture? Because God is almighty and can do them. Why do you believe that a Virgin conceived and bore a Son? Because it is God's act, and He can do anything. As the Angel Gabriel said to the Blessed Virgin, "No word is impossible with God." On the other hand, when holy Zacharias was told by the Angel that the old Elizabeth, his wife, should conceive, he said, "Whence shall I know this?" and he was punished at once for disbelieving. Why do you believe that our Lord rose from the dead? Why, that He redeemed us all with His precious blood? Why, that He washes away our sins in Baptism? Why do you believe in the power and grace which attends the other sacraments? Why do you believe in the resurrection of our bodies? You believe it because nothing is too hard for God—because however wonderful a thing may be, He can do it. Why do you believe in the virtue of holy relics? Why do you believe that the Saints hear your prayers? Because nothing is too hard for the Lord.

This especially applies to the great miracle of the Altar. Why do you believe that the Priest changes the bread into the body of Christ? Because God is almighty and nothing is too hard for Him. And moreover you know, as I have said, that miracles are the signs and tokens of God's presence. If then He is present in the Catholic Church, it is *natural* to expect that He will work some miracles, and if He did no miracle, we might be almost tempted to believe that He had left His Church.

When you assist at the holy sacrifice of the Altar and bow down at the elevation, and whenever you make an act of faith in God, steadily contemplating all that He has done for us in the Gospel, recollect God is almighty, and it will enable you to be bolder and more determined in making it. Say, I believe this and that, because God is almighty—I do not worship a creature: I am not the servant of a God of restricted power. But since God can *do* everything, I can *believe* everything. There is nothing too much for Him to do, and nothing too hard for me to believe. I will enlarge my heart. I will go forward in a generous way. "Open thy mouth wide," says God to me, "and I will fill it." Well, I do open my mouth, I desire to be fed with His words. I desire to live and to thrive by every word which He speaks. I desire to say with the prophet, "Speak, Lord, for thy servant heareth." I will not grudge, I will not doubt, because I believe that which takes away all doubting. All acts of divine power do but fall under, and are but instances of, that universal attribute on which

25

I believe, omnipotence. If God can do all things, He can do this. He can do much more than this. Wonderful as this or that may be to our narrow minds, still if we knew all, we should see that this, whatever it is, was but one thing out of many. This is what our Lord signified to holy Nathanael. Nathanael, struck with something which our Lord said, cried out, "Rabbi, Thou art the Son of God, Thou art the King of Israel." He made answer "Believest thou on this account? thou shalt see a greater thing than this." There is no end of God's power; it is inexhaustible. Let there be no end to our faith. Let us not be startled at what we are called on to believe; let us still be on the look out. Some people are slow to believe the miracles ascribed to the Saints. Now we know that such miracles are not part of the *faith*; they have no place in the Creed. And some are reported on better evidence than others. Some may be true, and others not so certainly true. Others again may be true but not miracles. But still why should they be *surprised* to hear of miracles? Are they beyond the power of God, and is not God present with the Saints, and has He not wrought miracles of old? Are miracles a new thing? There is no reason to be surprised, on the contrary; because in the Sacrifice of the Mass He works daily the most wonderful of miracles at the word of the priest. If then He does daily a miracle greater than any that can be named, why should we be surprised to hear reports of His doing other and lesser miracles now and then?

The Gospel of the day then sets before us the duty of *faith*, and rests it upon God's almightiness or omnipotence, as it is called. Nothing is too hard for Him, and we believe what the Church tells us of His deeds and providences, because He can do whatsoever He will. But there is another grace which the Gospel teaches us, and that is *hope* or *trust*. You observe that when the storm came, the disciples were in great *distress*. They thought some great calamity was coming on them. Therefore Christ said to them, "Why are ye *fearful*?" Hope and fear are contrary to each other; they feared because they did not hope. To hope is, not only to believe in God, but to believe and be certain that He loves us and means well to us; and therefore it is a great Christian grace. For faith without hope is not certain to bring us to Christ. The devils believe and tremble (Jas 2:19). They believe, but they do not come to Christ—because they do not hope, but despair. They despair of getting any good from Him. Rather they know that they shall get nothing but evil, so they keep away. You recollect the man possessed of the devil said: "What have we to do with Thee, Jesus the Son of God—art Thou come hither to torment us before the time?" (Matt 8:29). The coming of Christ was no comfort to them, the contrary: they shrank from Him. They knew He meant them not good, but punishment. But to men He meant good, and it is by knowing and feeling this that men are brought to Him. They will not come to God till they are sure of this. They must believe that He is not only almighty, but all merciful also. Faith is founded on the knowledge that God is almighty, hope is founded on the knowledge that God is all merciful. And the presence of our Lord and Saviour Jesus Christ excites us to hope quite as much as to faith, because His very name Jesus means Saviour, and because He was so loving, meek, and bountiful when He was on earth.

He said to the disciples when the storm arose, "Why are ye *fearful?*" That is, you ought to hope, you ought to trust, you ought to repose your heart on Me. I am not only almighty, but I am all merciful. I have come on earth because I am most loving to you. Why am I here, why am I in human flesh, why have I these hands which I stretch out to you, why have I these eyes from which the tears of pity flow, except that I wish you well, that I wish to save you? The storm cannot hurt you if *I* am with you. Can you be better placed than under my protection? Do you doubt My power or My will, do you think Me *negligent* of you that I sleep in the ship, and *unable* to help you except I am awake? Wherefore do you doubt? Wherefore do you fear? Have I been so long with you, and you do not yet trust Me, and cannot remain in peace and quiet by My side?"

And so, my Brethren, He says to us now. All of us who live in this mortal life, have our troubles. You have your troubles, but when you are in trouble, and the waves seem to mount high, and to be soon to overwhelm you, make an act of faith, an act of hope, in your God and Saviour. He calls you to Him who has His mouth and His hands full of blessings for you. He says: "Come unto Me, all that labour and are laden, and I will refresh you" (Matt 11:28). "All ye that thirst," He cries out by His prophet, "come ye to the waters, and ye that have no money, haste ye, buy, and eat." Never let the thought come into your mind that God is a hard master, a severe master. It is true the day will come when He will come as a just Judge, but now is the time of mercy. Improve it and make the most of the time of grace. "Behold now is the acceptable time, behold now is the day of salvation." This is the day of hope, this is the day of work, this is the day of activity. "The night cometh when no man can work," but we are children of the light and of the day, and therefore despondency, cold-ness of heart, fear, sluggishness are sins in us. Temptations indeed come on you to murmur, but resist them, drive them aside, pray God to help you with His mighty grace. He allows no temptation to befall us which He does not give us grace to surmount. Do not let your hope give way, but "lift up the languid hands and the relaxed knees" (Heb 12:12). "Lose not your confidence, which hath a great reward" (Heb 10:35). Seek His face who ever dwells in real and bodily presence in His Church. Do at least as much as what the disciples did. They had but little faith, they feared, they had not any great confidence and peace, but at least they did not keep away from Christ. They did not sit still sullenly, but they came to Him. Alas, our very best state is not higher than the Apostles' worst state. Our Lord blamed them as having *little* faith, because they cried out to Him. I wish we Christians of this day did as much as this. I wish we went as far as to cry out to Him in alarm. I wish we had only as much faith and hope as that which Christ thought so little in His first disciples. At least imitate the apostles in their weakness, if you can't imitate them in their strength. If you can't act as saints, at least act as Christians. Do not keep from Him, but, when you are in trouble, come to Him day by day asking Him earnestly and perseveringly for those favours which He alone can give. And as He on this occasion spoken of in the Gospel, blamed indeed the disciples, but did for them what they asked, so, (we will trust in His great mercy), though He discerns much infirmity in you which ought not to be there, yet He will deign to rebuke the winds and the sea, and say "Peace, be still," and there will be a great calm.

May this be your happy lot, my dear Brethren, and may the blessing of God Almighty, the Father, etc.

PREPARATION FOR THE JUDGMENT

Septuagesima,
20th February, 1848

THE LAST shall be first and the first last, for many are called, but few are chosen. Such are the words with which the Gospel of this day ends, which is the Parable of the Labourers in the Vineyard. In that parable, you know well, my Brethren, the Master of the Vineyard calls into his Vineyard all the labourers he can get together. He calls them in at different times, some in the morning, some at noon, some shortly before the evening. When the evening is come, he bids his paymaster call them together and give them their wages for the day past. It is very plain what this means. The Master of the Vineyard is our Lord and Saviour. We are the labourers. The evening is the hour of death, when we shall each receive the reward of our labour, if we have laboured well.

There is more in the parable than this, but I shall not go into the details of it. I shall here content myself with the general sketch I have taken of it, and with the words with which it concludes, "The last shall be first and the first last, for," etc.

Well is the hour of death described as the evening. There is something in the evening especially calm and solemn, fitly representing the hour of death. How peculiar, how unlike anything else, is a summer evening, when after the fever and heat of the day, after walking, or after working, after any toil, we cease from it, and for a few minutes enjoy the grateful feeling of rest! Especially is it so in the country, where evening tends to fill us with peace and tranquillity. The decreasing light, the hushing of all sounds, the sweet smell, perhaps, of the woods or the herbs which are all about us, the mere act of resting, and the consciousness that night is coming, all tend to tranquillize us and make us serious. Alas, I know that in persons of irreligious mind it has a very different effect, and while other men are raised to the love of God and Christ and the thought of heaven by the calm evening, *they* are but led to the thought of evil and deeds of sin. But I am speaking of those who live towards God and train their hearts heavenward, and I say that such persons find in the calm evening but an incitement to greater devotion, greater renunciation of the world. It does but bring before them the coming down of death, and leads them with the Apostle to die daily. Evening is the time for divine visitations. The Lord God visited Adam after he had sinned in the garden, in the cool of the evening. In the evening the patriarch Isaac went out to meditate in the field. In the evening our Lord discovered Himself to the two disciples who went to Emmaus. In the same evening He appeared to the Eleven, breathed on them, gave them the Holy Ghost, and invested them with the power of remitting and retaining sins.

Nay even in a town the evening is a soothing time. It is soothing to be at the end of the week, having completed the week's work, with the day of rest before us. It is soothing, even after the day of rest, though labour is in store for us against the morrow, to find ourselves in the evening of the day. It is a feeling that almost all must be able to bear witness to, as something peculiar, as something fitly prefiguring that awful time when our work will be done, and we shall rest from our labours.

That indeed will be emphatically our evening, when the long day of life is over and eternity is at hand. Man goeth forth to his work and to his labour until the evening, and then the night cometh when no man can work. There is something inexpressibly solemn and subduing in that time, when work is done and judgement is coming. O my brethren, we must each of us in his turn, sooner or later, arrive at that hour. Each of us must come to the evening of life. Each of us must enter on eternity. Each of us must come to that quiet, awful time, when we appear before the Lord of the Vineyard, and answer for the deeds done in the body, whether they be good or bad. That, my dear brethren, you will have to undergo. Every one of you must undergo the particular judgement, and it will be the stillest, awfullest time which you ever can experience. It will be the dread moment of expectation, when your fate for eternity is in the balance, and when you are about to be sent forth the companion of saints or devils without possibility of change. There can be no change, there can be no reversal. As that judgement decides it, so it will be for ever and ever. Such is the particular judgement. The general judgement at the end of the world will be a time of dreadful publicity, and will be full of the terrible brightness of the Judge. The trump of the Archangel will sound, and the Lord will descend from heaven in lightning. The graves will open. The sun and the moon will be darkened and this earth will pass away. This is not the time of evening, but rather it will be a tempest in the midst of the night. But the parable in the Gospel speaks of the time of evening, and by the evening is meant, not the end of the world, but the time of death. And really perhaps it will be as awful, though very different, that solitary judgement, when the soul stands before its Maker, to answer for itself. O who can tell which judgement is the more terrible, the silent secret judgement, or the open glorious coming of the Judge. It will be most terrible certainly, and it comes first, to find ourselves by ourselves, one by one, in His presence, and to have brought before us most vividly all the thoughts, words and deeds of this past life. Who will be able to bear the sight of himself? And yet we shall be obliged steadily to confront ourselves and to see ourselves. In this life we shrink from knowing our real selves. We do not like to know how sinful we are. We love those who prophesy smooth things to us, and we are angry with those who tell us of our faults. But then, not one fault only, but all the secret, as well as evident, defects of our character will be clearly brought out. We shall see what we feared to see here, and much more. And then, when the full sight of ourselves comes to us, who will not wish that he had known more of himself here, rather than leaving it for the inevitable day to reveal it all to him!

I am speaking, not only of the bad, but of the good. Those indeed who have died in neglect of good, it will be a most insufferably dreadful sight to them, and they will not have long to contemplate it, in silence, for they will be hurried away to their punishment. But I speak of holy souls, souls that will be saved, and I say that to these the sight of themselves will be intolerable, and it will be a torment to them to see what they really are and the sins which lie against them. And hence some writers have said that their horror will be such that of their own will, and from a holy indignation against themselves, they will be ready to plunge into Purgatory in order to satisfy divine justice, and to be clear of what is to their own clear sense and spiritual judgement so abominable. We do not know how great an evil sin is. We do not know how subtle and penetrating an evil it is. It circles round us and enters in every seam, or rather at every pore. It is like dust covering everything, defiling every part of us, and requiring constant attention, constant cleansing. Our very duties cover us with this miserable dust and dirt. As we labour in God's vineyard and do His will, the while from the infirmity of our nature we sin in lesser matters even when we do good in greater, so that when the evening comes, with all our care, in spite of the sacraments of the Church, in spite of our prayers and our penance, we are covered with the heat and defilement of the day.

This, I say, will be the case even with religious persons who have laboured to save their souls; but Oh! how miserable will be the case of those who have never had religious thoughts! There are persons, for instance, who cannot bear thought of any kind, who cannot bear an hour's silent reflection. It would be a great punishment to many a man to be obliged to think of himself. Many men like to live in a whirl, in some excitement or other which keeps their minds employed, and keeps them from thinking of themselves. How many a man, e.g. employs all his leisure time in learning merely the news of the day. He likes to read the periodical publications, he likes to know what is going on in the four quarters of the earth. He fills his mind with matters which either do not concern him, or concern only his temporal welfare; with what they are doing in various parts of England, what Parliament is doing, what is done in Ireland, what is done on the Continent; nay he descends to little matters of no importance, rather than entertain that thought which must come on him, if not before, at least in the evening of life and when he stands before his Judge. Others are full of projects for making money; be they high or be they low, that is their pursuit, they covet wealth and they live in the thought how they may get it. They are alive to inventions and improvements in their particular trade, and to nothing else. They rival each other. They as it were, run a race with each other, not a heavenly race, such as the Apostle's who ran for a crown incorruptible, but a low earthly race, each trying by all means in his power to distance his neighbour in what is called the favour of the public, making this their one end, and thinking nothing at all of religion. And others take up some doctrine whether of politics or of trade or of philosophy, and spend their lives upon it; they go about to recommend it in every way they can. They speak, they write, they labour for an object which will perish with this world, which cannot pass with them through the grave. The holy Apostle says "Blessed are they that die in the Lord, for their works do *follow them*" (Apoc 14:13). Good works follow us, bad works follow us, but everything else is worth nothing; everything else is but chaff. The whirl and dance of worldy matters is but like the whirling of chaff or dust, nothing comes of it; it lasts through the day, but it is not to be found in the evening. And yet how many immortal souls spend their lives in nothing better than making themselves giddy with this whirl of politics, of party, or religious opinion, or money getting, of which nothing can ever come.

Observe in the parable the Master of the Vineyard did but one thing. He told his servant to "call the labourers and give them their hire." He did but ask *what they had done*. He did not ask what their opinion was about science, or about art, or about the means of wealth, or about public affairs; he did not ask them if they knew the nature of the vine for which they had been labouring. They were not required to know how many kinds of vines there were in the world, and what countries vines could grow in, and where they could not. They were not called upon to give their opinion what soils were best for the vines. They were not examined in the minerals, or the shrubs, or in anything else which was found in the vineyard, but this was the sole question, whether they had *worked* in the vineyard. First they must be in the vineyard, then they must work in it; these were the two things. So will it be with us after death. When we come into God's presence, we shall be asked two things, whether we were in the Church, and whether we worked in the Church. Everything else is worthless. Whether we have been rich or poor, whether we have been learned or unlearned, whether we have been prosperous or afflicted, whether we have been sick or well, whether we have had a good name or a bad one, all this will be far from the work of that day. The single question will be, are we Catholics and are we good Catholics? If we have not been, it will avail nothing that we have been ever so honoured here, ever so successful, have had ever so good a name. And if we have been, it will matter nothing though we have been ever so despised, ever so poor, ever so hardly pressed, ever so troubled, ever so unfriended. Christ will make up everything to us, if we have been faithful to Him; and He will take everything away from us, if we have lived to the world.

Then will be fulfilled the awful words of the parable. Many that are last shall be first, for many are called but few are chosen. Then, also, will it be seen how many have received grace and have not profited by it. Then will be seen how many were called, called by the influence of God's grace, called into the Church, yet how few have a place prepared in heaven. Then will be seen how many resisted their conscience, resisted the call of Christ to follow Him, and so are lost. This is the day both of divine grace and of patience. God gives grace and is patient with us, but when death comes, there is no more time either for grace or for patience. Grace is exhausted, patience is exhausted. Nothing remains but judgement, a terrible judgement on those who have lived in disobedience.

And oh! what a sight it will be, what an unexpected sight, at the last day and public judgement to be present at that revelation of all hearts! How different persons will then seem, from what they seem now! How will the last be first, and the first last! Then those whom the world looked up to, will be brought low, and those who were little esteemed, will be exalted. Then will it be found who are the real movers in the world's affairs, those who sustained the cause of the Church or who influenced the fortunes of empires, were not the great and powerful, not those whose names are known in the world, but the humble despised followers of the Lamb, the meek saint, the man full of prayer and good works whom the world passed by; the hidden band of saintly witnesses, whose voice day by day ascended to Christ; the sufferers who seemed to be living for nothing; the poor whom the proud world thought but an offence and a nuisance. When that Day comes, may it reveal good for each of you, my brethren, and may the blessing, etc.

THE CALLS OF GRACE

Septuagesima,
27th February, 1848

IN THE PARABLE of the Sower, which has formed the Gospel for this day, we have set before us four descriptions of men, all of whom receive the word of God. The sower sows first on the hard ground or road, then on the shallow earth or rock, then on a ground where other seeds were sown, and lastly on really good, rich, well-prepared soil. By the sower is meant the preacher; and by the seed the word preached; and by the rock, the road, the preoccupied ground, and the good soil, are meant four different states of mind of those who hear the word. Now here we have a picture laid out before us, which will, through God's mercy, provide us with a fitting subject of thought this evening.

First let us consider the case of the hard ground and the seed that was sown there—"some fell by the road and was trodden down and the birds of the heaven ate it up." Such is the power of the divine word, spoken by its appointed preacher; so blessed and prospered is it by divine grace, that it goes forth like a dart or an arrow. Amos the prophet says: "Their arrows are very sharp, in the heart of the King's enemies"; and another prophet says: "I have hewn them by the prophet. I have slain them with the words of My mouth." And so in the book of the Apocalypse we read of our Lord as represented with a sharp sword out of his mouth; and St. Paul speaks of the sword of the Spirit which is the Word of God. The word goeth forth, as the prophet Isaias says, and does not return unto Him void, but prospers in the thing whereto He sends it. Nothing can stop it, but a closed heart. Nothing can resist it, but a deliberately worldly, carnal and godless will—and such a will can. But where the heart is ever so little softened, the divine word enters it; where it is not softened, it lies on the surface. It lies on the surface and we learn from the parable the immediate consequence: "the birds of the air stole it away." It did not lie there long. There was but the alternative—it was admitted within, or the wind or the birds or the foot of the passer-by, as it might be, destroyed it.

Now I can fancy some of those who hear me thinking that this is an extreme case—when perhaps it is their own. When they read or hear this picture of the seed falling on the hard wayside, they may hear it in an unconcerned way, as if they had not interest in it, when they may have a great concern in the description. There are a very great many persons whose hearts are like the hard wayside. Now I will explain what I mean. I suppose it occurs to all of us to hear names of persons mentioned, or to hear of events, or occurrences, which we hear one moment and forget the next: they simply pass through our minds and make no impression. Why? Because we never heard of them before; we take no interest in them, and so they don't take hold of us. They are like an unknown language, and go as they came. But now supposing the person mentioned is one whose history we know. Supposing it is a public man, whom we have heard about or read of for years—Why, did we hear of anything happening to him, did we hear he had left the country, or fallen into misfortune, or fallen ill, or been promoted, or had died, his name kindles up a whole history, and we take great interest in the news brought us. We connect what we now hear with what we already know. And so you often may find, coming into a party of men, and saying this or that of a certain person, that the news produces a great effect on one, and is simply unmeaning to another. The latter turns off to some other subject at once, and is not struck, but the former expresses surprise, or pleasure or grief, and says: "Is it possible?" "I remember such a man twenty years ago—how he is changed, or how great a rise, or what a sad end." We might hear, as just now, that the king of the French has abdicated. One man says "I recollect his coming to the throne," and he will muse on it. To another the news is so many idle words, and he thinks nothing of it.

And much more—if the news concerned some dear friend, or some near relation. Did we hear even his name mentioned in conversation, our ears are so sharp that we should catch it at once; because the image of a person whom we know well is associated in our minds with a thousand thoughts—he has a place in us—he is, as it were, part of us. He has a long history written within us; his name has a deep meaning.

But you see the difference between one whose heart is hard, and one whose heart is softened. One man has often thought about religion, another never. The latter will be interested enough if you speak to him of things connected with this world, if you talk only of how to raise crops or how to make money in any way, or of any worldly amusement or pleasure, his attention is arrested at once. But if you speak to him about the four last things, about heaven or hell, death or judgement, he stares or laughs out. If you speak good and holy words to him, he hears and forgets. This is the dreadful case with many at death; religious persons say what they can to touch the dying man and the poor patient hears indeed, but hears without emotion, without thought of any kind. The words fall off, and have no effect—and so he dies. On the contrary some sacred place or sacred name is like a magic spell to those whose hearts are accustomed to the thought of religion, or are in any way disposed and prepared by God's grace. Take a person who has been tried by misfortune, or who has suffered the loss of some dear relative, or who has fallen into sin and is under compunctions, then when he hears the words "What shall I do to be saved?" or "After death, the judgement," or "believe and be saved," or "Comfort ye, comfort ye, my people," or "Christ died for sinners,"— such few words fit into his habitual state of mind, and at once kindle him—he cannot help listening—he seizes the word and devours it. Nay we know that to holy people the very name of Jesus is a name to feed upon, a name to transport; or the name of Mary, or of both—"Jesu Mariae" and "Alma Redemptoris Mater"—Saints have gone into ecstasy upon the name. The picture, which it brings before the mind of Mother and Son, the Eternal Son and His high-favoured Mother, awful transporting relationship, most human yet most divine, these are the words which can raise the dead and transfigure and beatify the living.

You will observe that, in the parable, not only did the fowls carry off the word of life, but the foot of the passer-by trampled it. I have hitherto spoken of those who were ignorant, careless and heartless, and from whom the devil stole the divine treasure, while they let it lie on the surface of their minds. But there are others who are worse than this; who, as it were, trample on the divine words. Such are those who feel a disdain and hatred of the truth. It is an awful thing to say, but we see it before our eyes how many people there are who hate the doctrine which Christ revealed and the Church teaches. Of course many do so in mere ignorance, and would feel and act otherwise, if they had the opportunity. But there are those, and not a few, who scorn and are irritated at the preaching of the word of life, and spurn it from them. It has been so from the beginning. Cain slew Abel; Joseph was stripped and sold by his brethren; David was hated by Saul; and above all our Lord was spat upon and put to death by the Jews. "He came unto His own and His own received Him not." And as He was abominated and cast out by a sinful generation, so, since He has departed, His word is abominated by the world still. Sometimes it is for want of love. You hear people revile the Church, ridicule the most sacred things, get angry directly they are mentioned, frown and change countenance, nay shake all over when they see a priest, suspect everything that is shocking and detestable as the characteristic of monk or nun, and spread from a deep prejudice the most untrue stories. Sometimes from want of faith; they think it quite wonderful, beyond expression strange and marvellous, that men can be found to believe this or that doctrine; they won't believe they can; they think they pretend to believe what they don't; they look upon all educated Catholics as hypocrites—and sometimes it arises from a bad conscience and impatience at being told their duty. Our Lord bids us not cast our pearls before swine, but they trample them under their feet. This is what carnal, sensual people do. They wish to live their own way; they do not like to be warned of hell and judgement, and when the warning voice comes to them, they rise up against it, and think it a personal offence to themselves that it declares the truth of God. They put their foot upon it, and tread out the heavenly flame.

But I will now go on to mention a third case of hardness of heart, which not infrequently occurs, and that is, the case of those who get familiar with the word of life and then are not moved by it. When persons who are living in sin hear for the first time the sound of Catholic truth, they are affected by it; it is something new and the novelty of the doctrine is God's instrument. It is blest by God, to make an effect upon them. It moves and draws them. And then the worship of the Catholic Church is so overcoming—the holy forms, the sacred actions, the awful functions (Benediction, for instance), subdue them. They, as it were, give up, they surrender themselves to God, they feel themselves in the hands of their Saviour. They are led to cry out: "Take me, make what Thou wilt of me." This lasts for some time, and in a number of cases, praised be God, it ends happily; this excitement and transport of mind leads on to a lasting conversion. But in other cases it does not. A person is moved for a while, and then the excitement goes off. I have seen cases of this kind—many people may know them. A man is on the point of making a real conversion; he is on the point of taking up religion seriously. He is on the point of putting one and one object alone before him as the end of his being and the aim of his life, to please God and save his soul. But all of a sudden a change comes over him. Almost while we turn our head and look another way, it has taken place. We look back to him and he is quite another man—or rather he is the same, the same as he was. He has lapsed into his old forgetfulness of religion, and when he has once relaxed, it is impossible to move him. There he is for ever. And so, when a person is not exactly forgetful of religion, but has a form of religion; lives by rule and is called, and in a certain way is, a religious man; but is at one time moved to embrace that one true form of godliness which comes from heaven, putting aside his idols and vanities; *if* he neglects to take the step, *if* his courage fails him, or his pride stops him, or love of the world draws him back, and he gives up the notion, he is not what he was before. No, for he is worse. The latter state of that man is worse than the first. He was hard before, and now is he ten times as hard. Not only the good seed has been trampled on, but his heart has been trodden down; it is as hard as the pavement, and nothing will move him again.

This, alas, is often the case in places where truth has been preached for many years, compared with new places. In the new place you find the word prospers; but there is coldness, deadness, languor, tepidity, backwardness, insincerity, in the old.

There is a case of this hardness of heart still more awful. I have known the case of a person taking up religion for a time and seeming to be religious and then casting it off, and giving up even the belief in God, just like a brute of the field; and confessing it, confessing it in language such as this:—"I was religious once. Religion had its day with me. It grew up, like the grass, and it has come to nought like the grass. I can't revive it. It was a certain state of mind of a certain period of my life, but I have outgrown it."

And now, my dear Brethren, what other lesson can I draw from these considerations, than that which the Prophet gives us in the Psalm, and which the Apostle borrows from him: "Today if ye shall hear His voice, harden not your hearts, as in the provocation, according to the day of temptation in the wilderness ... Exhort one another every day whilst it is called today, lest any be hardened by the deceitfulness of sin" (Heb 3:8, 13). When the heart is hard, the birds take away the divine seed. They do not bring it back; it goes for ever. Make the most of the precious time. Delay not—many a soul has been damned by delay. God's opportunities do not wait; they come and they go. The word of life waits not—if it is not appropriated by you, the devil will appropriate. He delays not, but has his eyes wide always and is ready to pounce down and carry off the gift which you delay to use.

And if you are conscious that your hearts are hard, and are desirous that they should be softened, do not despair. All things are possible to you, through God's grace. Come to Him for the will and the power to do that to which He calls you. He never forsakes anyone who calls upon him. He never puts any trial on a man but He gives Him grace to overcome it. Do not despair then; nay do not despond, even though you do come to Him, yet are not at once exalted to overcome yourselves. He gives grace by little and little. It is by coming daily into His presence, that by degrees we find ourselves awed by that presence and able to believe and obey Him. Therefore if any one desires illumination to know God's will as well as strength to do it, let him come to Mass daily, if he possibly can. At least let him present himself daily before the Blessed Sacrament, and, as it were, offer his heart to His Incarnate Saviour, presenting it as a reasonable offering to be influenced, changed and sanctified under the eye and by the grace of the Eternal Son. And let him every now and then through the day make some short prayer or ejaculation, to the Lord and Saviour, and again to His Blessed Mother, the immaculate most Blessed Virgin Mary, or again to his guardian Angel, or to his Patron Saint. Let him now and then collect his mind and place himself, as if in heaven, in the presence of God; as if before God's throne; let him fancy he sees the All-Holy Lamb of God, which taketh away the sin of the world. These are the means by which, with God's grace, he will be able in course of time to soften his heart—not all at once, but by degrees; not by his own power or wisdom, but by the grace of God blessing his endeavour. Thus it is that Saints have begun. They have begun by these little things, and so become at length Saints. They were not saints all at once, but by little and little. And so we, who are not saints, must still proceed by the same road; by lowliness, patience, trust in God, recollection that we are in His presence, and thankfulness for His mercies.

And now, my Brethren, though I have said but a little on a large subject, I have said enough, not enough for the subject, but enough for you, enough for you to get a lesson from. May you lay it to heart, as I am sure you do and will, may you gain a blessing from it; and in this as in all things may the blessing of God Almighty, the Father, etc.

Prejudice and Faith

Quinquagesima,
15th March, 1848

WE HAVE in the Gospel for this day what, I suppose, has raised the wonder of most readers of the New Testament. I mean the slowness of the disciples to take in the notion that our Lord was to suffer on the Cross. It can only be accounted for by the circumstance that a contrary opinion had strong possession of their minds—what we call a strong prejudice against the truth, in their cases an honest religious prejudice, the prejudice of honest religious minds, but still a deep and violent prejudice. When our Lord first declared it, St. Peter said, "Be it far from thee, Lord, this shall not happen to Thee." He spoke so strongly that the holy Evangelist says that he "took our Lord and began to rebuke Him." He did it out of reverence and love, as the occasion of it shows, but still that he spoke with warmth, with vehemence, is evident from the expression. Think then how deep his prejudice must have been.

This same prejudice accounts for what we find in today's gospel. Our Lord said, "Behold we go to Jerusalem, and all that is written of the Son of man shall be accomplished. For He shall be delivered to the Gentiles, and shall be mocked and scourged and spat upon; and after they have scourged Him, they will put Him to death, and the third day He shall rise again." Could words be plainer? Yet what effect had they on the disciples? "They understood none of these things, and this was hid from them, and they understood not the things that were said." Why hid? Because they had not eyes to see.

And so again after the resurrection, when they found the sepulchre empty, it is said, "They knew not the Scripture, that He must rise again from the dead." And when St. Mary Magdalen and the other women told them, "their words seemed to them as an idle tale, and they did not believe them"; and accordingly when our Lord appeared to them, "He upbraided them with their incredulity and hardness of heart, because they did not believe them who had seen Him after He was risen again."

This is certainly a very remarkable state of mind, and the record of it in the gospels may serve to explain much which goes on among us, and to put us on our guard against ourselves, and to suggest to us the question, Are we in any respect in the same state of imperfection as these holy, but at that time prejudiced, disciples of our Lord and Saviour?

It will be well to observe what the cause of their blindness was—it was a false interpretation which they had given to the Old Testament Scriptures, an interpretation which was common in their day, and which they had been taught by the Scribes and Pharisees, who sat in Moses' seat and pretended to teach them Moses' doctrine. It was the opinion of numbers at that day that the promised Messiah or Christ, who was coming, would be a great temporal Prince, like Solomon, only greater; that he was to have an earthly court, earthly wealth, earthly palaces, lands and armies and servants and the glory of a temporal kingdom. This was their idea—they looked for a deliverer, but thought he would come like Gideon, David, or Judas Maccabaeus, with sword and spear and loud trumpet, inflicting wounds and shedding blood, and throwing his captives into dungeons.

And they fancied Scripture taught this doctrine. They took parts of Scripture which pleased their fancy, in the first place, and utterly put out of their minds such as went contrary to these. It is quite certain that the Prophet Isaias and other prophets speak of our Lord, then to come, as a conqueror. He speaks of Him as red with the blood of His enemies, and smiting in wrath the heads of diverse countries; as ruling kings with a rod of iron, and extending His dominion to the ends of the earth. It is also true that Scripture elsewhere speaks of the Messias otherwise. He is spoken of as rejected of men, as a leper, as an outcast, as persecuted, as spat upon and pierced and slain. But these passages they put away from them. They did not let them produce their legitimate effects upon their hearts. They heard them with the ear and not with the head, and so it was all one as if they had not been written; to them they were not written. It did not occur to them that they possibly could mean, what nevertheless they did mean. Therefore, when our Lord told them that He, He the Christ, was to be scourged and spat upon, they were taken by surprise, and they cried out, "Be it far from Thee, Lord—impossible, that Thou, the Lord of glory, should be buffeted and bruised, wounded and killed. This shall not happen unto Thee."

You see that the mistake of the Apostles, and their horror and rejection of what nevertheless was the Eternal and most blessed Truth of the gospel, arose from a religious zeal for the honour of God; though a false zeal. It were well, if the similar mistake of people nowadays had so excellent a source and so good an excuse. For, so it is, that now as then, men are to be found who, with Scripture in their hands, in their memories, and in their mouths, yet make great mistakes as to the meaning of it, and that because they are prejudiced against the true sense of it.

"I speak as to win men" as the Apostle says; "Judge ye what I say." Is it not so, my dear Brethren? Far be it from me to be severe with such, but is it not so, that in this educated and intelligent and great people, there are multitudes,—nay more, the great majority is such, as to have put a false sense on Scripture, and to be violently opposed to the truth on account of this false interpretation? The Church of Christ walks the earth now, as Christ did in the days of His flesh, and as our Lord fulfilled the Scriptures in what was and what He did then, so the Church fulfils the Scriptures in what she is and what she does now; as Christ was promised, predicted, in the Scriptures as He was then, so is the Church promised, predicted, in the Scriptures in what she is now. Yet the people of this day, though they read the Scriptures and think they understand them, like the Jews then, who read the Scriptures and thought they understood them, do not understand them. Why? Because like the Jews then, they have been taught badly; they have received false traditions, as the Jews had received the traditions of the Pharisees, and are blind when they think they see, and are prejudiced against the truth, and shocked and offended when they are told it.

And, as the Jews then passed over passages in Scripture,

which ought to have set them right, so do Christians now pass over passages, which would, if dwelt on, extricate them from their error. For example, the Jews passed over the texts: "They pierced my hands and my feet," "My God, My God, why hast Thou forsaken Me?" "He was rejected of men, a man of sorrows and acquainted with grief,"—which speak of Christ. And men nowadays pass over such passages as the following which speak of the Church: "Whosesoever sins ye remit, they are remitted to them"; "Thou art Peter and upon this rock I will build my Church"; "Anointing them with oil in the Name of the Lord"; "The Church the pillar and foundation of the truth"; and the like. They are so certain that the doctrine of the one Holy Catholic Church is not true, that they will not give their mind to these passages, they pass them over. They cannot tell you what they mean, but they are quite sure they do not mean what Catholics say they mean, because Catholicism is not true. In fact a deep prejudice is on their minds, or what Scripture calls blindness. They cannot tell what these passages and many others mean, but they do not care. They say that after all they are not important—which is just begging the question—and when they are urged and forced to give them a meaning, they say any thing that comes uppermost, merely to satisfy or to perplex the questioner, wishing nothing more than to get rid of what they think a troublesome, but idle, question.

Now is it not strange that persons who act in this way, who skip over things in Scripture, and go by their prejudices, and by the bad teaching they have received in Scripture, should yet boast that they are scriptural and go by Scripture, and use their private judgement? No, they do not judge, they do not examine, they do not go by Scripture; but they take just so much of Scripture as suits them, and leave the rest. They go, not by their private judgement, but their private prejudice, and by their private liking.

Now I will add one thing more. Persons who act thus are of very different character, just as those who stumbled at our Lord when He came on earth were very different from each other. Both the hard-hearted Pharisees and the tender-hearted Apostles were surprised and shocked at Christ's Passion and death. And so now two sorts of persons are offended at the Holy Church—some are hopeless, other are hopeful. The event shows it. We cannot decide which are the one, which the other, except by the event; but so it is—some are driven further and further from the Church, the more they hear and see of it, and others as time goes on are brought nearer to it, and submit themselves to it.

This being the state of the case, how are we Catholics to behave ourselves to such prejudiced and erring persons? We should imitate our Lord and Master. He was most patient with them; He abounded in long-suffering. "A bruised reed did He not break, and smoking flax did He not quench." He did not argue, but He quietly led them on. He displayed His wonders to them. He gradually influenced them by His words and by His grace, and then enlightened them, till they believed all things. Till that Apostle, who doubted most stoutly of His resurrection, cried out, overcome, "My Lord and My God." So must we do now—so does the Church do now. Argument is well in its place, but it is not the chief thing. The chief thing is to win the mind, to melt the heart, to influence the will. This the Church does. After the pattern of her Divine Lord she draws us with cords of a man, with cords of love, with divine charity; "she hopeth all things, endureth all things," she opens the gates of her temple, she lights up her altars, she displays the Most Holy under the sacramental veil, she bursts forth into singing, till the wayward soul, overcome and subdued, says with the Patriarch, "It is enough—let me now die, for I have seen Thy Face; Nunc Dimittis, Lord now lettest Thou Thy servant depart in peace, for mine eyes have seen Thy salvation. I have heard of Thee with the hearing of the ear, but now mine eye seeth Thee." And, as our Lord after His resurrection opened the understanding of the disciples to understand the Scripture, so now are the hearts of men softened and enlightened, and they see that the Church fulfils all the prophecies about herself, all that is written in the Law, the Prophets, and the Psalms; and thus they fall down and worship, and confess that God is here of a truth.

Blessed are they who thus fall down and worship. Blessed are they whom the grace of God leads on to embrace the truth. Blessed who yield their minds to the gentle influences of the Holy Ghost, and stop not till He has brought them on to the haven. But, my Brethren, what I have been saying does not apply exclusively to this or that set of men, but belongs to us all. For all of us, not this or that man only, but all of us, Catholics or not, are led forward by God in a wonderful way—through a way of wonders, a way wonderful to us, a way marvellous, strange, startling, to our natural feelings and tastes, whatever our place in the Church may be. As faith is the fundamental grace which God gives us, so a trial of faith is the necessary discipline which He puts upon us. We cannot well have faith without an exercise of faith.

This is implied in the very passage which has given occasion to the remarks which I have been making. When the disciples shrank from His words about His own death and passion, what did He do? He met a blind man, and He took him and gave him sight. Why did He give him this special favour? He expressly tells us. He says, "Thy faith hath made thee whole." Here was a tacit rebuke of the slowness to believe in His own disciples and friends, all things are possible to him that believeth. This poor outcast is a lesson to you, O My own people. He puts you to shame. He has had faith in Me, while ye stumble at My word, and when I say a thing, answer "Be it far from Thee, Lord."

The office this day gives us another instance of the same great lesson. The Church reads today the history of the call of Abraham, and meditates upon his great act of obedience, in lifting up his knife to slay his son. Abraham, our father, is our great pattern of faith, and his faith was tried, first by being called on to leave his country and kindred, next by being told to sacrifice his dearly beloved Isaac. The first was trying enough, but what a stumbling-block the second might have been to faith less than his. If the disciples were shocked that the divine Antitype should be put to death, surely Abraham too had cause of offence that his own Isaac was to be struck down and slain by him, by his hand, by the hand of his father! Yet he went about the fulfilment of this command, as gravely, as quietly, as calmly, as if it was a mere ordinary action. Thus he showed his faith and gained the blessing.

Be sure, my Brethren, that this must be our way too. Never does God give faith, but He tries it, and none without faith can enter the kingdom of heaven. Therefore all ye who come to serve God, all ye who wish to save your souls, begin with making up your minds that you cannot do so, without a generous faith, a generous self-surrender;

without putting yourselves into God's hands, making no bargain with Him, not stipulating conditions, but saying "O Lord here I am—I will be whatever Thou wilt ask me—I will go whithersoever Thou sendest me—I will bear whatever Thou puttest upon me. Not in my own might or my own strength. My strength is very weakness—if I trust in myself more or less, I shall fail—but I trust in Thee—I trust and I know that Thou wilt aid me to do, what Thou callest on me to do—I trust and I know that Thou wilt never leave me nor forsake me. Never wilt Thou bring me into any trial, which Thou wilt not bring me through. Never will there be a failing on Thy part, never will there be a lack of grace. I shall have all and abound. I shall be tried: my reason will be tried, for I shall have to believe; my affections will be tried, for I shall have to obey Thee instead of pleasing myself; my flesh will be tried, for I shall have to bring it into subjection. But Thou art more to me than all other things put together. Thou canst make up to me all Thou takest from me and Thou wilt, for Thou wilt give to me Thyself. Thou wilt guide me."

SURRENDER TO GOD

First Sunday in Lent,
12th March, 1848

I SUPPOSE it has struck many persons as very remarkable, that in the latter times the strictness and severity in religion of former ages has been so much relaxed. There has been a gradual abandonment of painful duties which were formerly inforced upon all. Time was when all persons, to speak generally, abstained from flesh through the whole of Lent. There have been dispensations on this point again and again, and this very year there is a fresh one. What is the meaning of this? What are we to gather from it? This is a question worth considering. Various answers may be given, but I shall confine myself to one of them.

I answer that fasting is only one branch of a large and momentous duty, the subdual of ourselves to Christ. We must surrender to Him all we have, all we are. We must keep nothing back. We must present to Him as captive prisoners with whom He may do what He will, our soul and body, our reason, our judgement, our affections, our imagination, our tastes, our appetite. The great thing is to *subdue* ourselves; but as to the particular form in which the great precept of self-conquest and self-surrender is to be expressed, that depends on the person himself, and on the time or place. What is good for one age or person, is not good for another.

There are other instances of the same variation. For example, devotion to the Saints is a Catholic practice. It is founded on a clear Catholic doctrine, and the Catholic practice has been the same from the beginning. It could not possibly change. Yet it is certain that the prominent object of that devotion has varied at different times, varying now in the case of individuals, one person having a devotion to one saint, another to another; and in like manner it has varied in the Church at large—for example, quite at first the Martyrs, as was natural, took up this principal attention. It was natural, when their friends were dying daily under the sword or at the stake before their eyes, to direct their devotion in the first instance to their glorified spirits. But when a time of external peace was granted, then the thought of the Blessed Virgin took up its abode in the hearts of the faithful, and there was a greater devotion than before to her. And this thought of the Blessed Virgin has grown stronger and clearer and more influential in the minds of the Church. The devout servants of Mary were comparatively few in the first ages, now they are many.

Again, to take another instance, the present war with evil spirits would seem to be very different from what it was in former ages. They attack a civilized age in a more subtle way than they attack a rude age. We read in lives of saints and others of the evil spirit showing himself and fighting with them face to face, but now those subtle and experienced spirits find it is more to their purpose not to show themselves, or at least not so much. They find it their interest to let the idea of them die away from the minds of men, that being unrecognized, they may do the more mischief. And they assault men in a more subtle way—not grossly, in some broad temptation, which everyone can understand, but in some refined way they address themselves to our pride or self-importance, or love of money, or love of ease, or love of show, or our depraved reason, and thus have really the dominion over persons who seem at first sight to be quite superior to temptation.

Now apply these illustrations to the case in point. From what has been said it follows that you must not suppose that nothing is incumbent on us in the way of mortification, though you have not to fast so strictly as formerly. It is reasonable to think that some other duty of the same general kind, may take its place; and therefore the permission granted us in eating may be a suggestion to us to be more severe with ourselves on the other hand in certain other respects.

And this anticipation is confirmed by the history of our Lord's temptation in the wilderness. It *began*, you will observe, with an attempt on the part of the evil one to make Him break His fast improperly. It *began*, but it did not end there. It was but the first of three temptations, and the other two were more addressed to His mind, not His bodily wants. One was to throw Himself down from the pinnacle, the other the offer of all the kingdoms of the world. They were more subtle temptations. Now I have used the word "subtle" already, and it needs some explanation. By a subtle temptation or a subtle sin, I mean one which it is very difficult to find out. Everyone knows what it is to break the ten commandments, the first, the second, the third, and so on. When a thing is directly commanded, and the devil tempts us directly to break it, this is *not* a subtle temptation, but a broad and gross temptation. But there are a great many things wrong which are not so obviously wrong. They are wrong as leading to what is wrong or the consequence of what is wrong, or they are wrong because they are the very same thing as what is forbidden, but dressed up and looking differently. The human mind is very deceitful; when a thing is forbidden, a man does not like directly to do it, but he goes to work if he can to get at the forbidden end in some way. It is like a man who has to make for some place. First he attempts to go straight to it, but finds the way blocked up; then he goes round about it. At first you would not think he is going in the right direction; he sets off perhaps at a right angle, but he just makes one little bend, then another, till at length he gets to his point. Or still more it is like a sailing vessel at sea with the wind contrary, but tacking first this way, and then that, the mariners contrive at length to get to their destination. This then is a subtle sin, when it at first seems not to be a sin, but comes round to the same point as an open direct sin.

To take some examples. If the devil tempted one to go out into the highway and rob, this would be an open, bold temptation. But if he tempted one to do something unfair in the course of business, which was to one's neighbour's hurt and to one's own advantage, it would be a more subtle temptation. The man would still take what was his neighbour's, but his conscience would not be so much shocked. So equivocation is a more subtle sin than direct lying. In like manner a person who does not intoxicate himself, may eat too much. Gluttony is a more subtle sin than drunkenness, because it does not show so much. And again, sins of the soul are more subtle sins than sins of the body. Infidelity is a more subtle sin than licentiousness.

Even in our Blessed Lord's case the Tempter began by addressing himself to His bodily wants. He had fasted forty days, and afterwards was hungered. So the devil tempted Him to eat. But when He did not consent, then he went on to more subtle temptations. He tempted Him to spiritual pride, and he tempted Him by ambition for power. Many a man would shrink from intemperance, of being proud of his spiritual attainments; that is, he would confess such things were wrong, but he would not see that he was guilty of them.

Next I observe that a civilized age is more exposed to subtle sins than a rude age. Why? For this simple reason, because it is more fertile in excuses and evasions. It can defend error, and hence can blind the eyes of those who have not very careful consciences. It can make error plausible, it can make vice look like virtue. It dignifies sin by fine names; it calls avarice proper care of one's family, or industry, it calls pride independence, it calls ambition greatness of mind; resentment it calls proper spirit and sense of honour, and so on.

Such is this age, and hence our self-denial must be very different from what was necessary for a rude age. Barbarians lately converted, or warlike multitudes, of fierce spirit and robust power—nothing can tame them better than fasting. But we are very different. Whether from the natural course of centuries or from our mode of living, from the largeness of our towns or other causes, so it is that our powers are weak and we cannot bear what our ancestors did. Then again what numbers there are who anyhow must have dispensation, whether because their labour is so hard, or because they never have enough, and cannot be called on to stint themselves in Lent. These are reasons for the rule of fasting not being so strict as once it was. And let me now say, that the rule which the Church now gives us, though indulgent, yet is strict too. It tries a man. One meal a day is trial to most people, even though on some days meat is allowed. It is sufficient, with our weak frames, to be a mortification of sensuality. It serves that end for which all fasting was instituted. On the other hand its being so light as it is, so much lighter than it was in former times, is a suggestion to us that there are other sins and weaknesses to mortify in us besides gluttony and drunkenness. It is a suggestion to us, while we strive to be pure and undefiled in our bodies, to be on our guard lest we are unclean and sinful in our intellects, in our affections, in our wills.

When the old rude age of the world was just ended, and an age which is called light and civilization had begun—I mean in the 16th century—the Providence of Almighty God raised up two saints. One came from Florence, and the other came from Spain, and they met together in Rome. They were as unlike each other as any two men could be, unlike in their history, in their character, in the religious institutes, which ultimately, by God's all-directing grace they were prospered in founding. The Spaniard had been a soldier—his history was exciting. He had been tossed about the world, and, after his conversion he founded a company of spiritual knights or cavaliers, as they may be called, who were bound to a sort of military service to the Holy See. The Florentine had been a saint from a boy, perhaps he never committed a mortal sin, and he was a stationary, home saint. For sixty years he lived in Rome and never left it. St. Philip Neri is the Florentine, and St. Ignatius is the Spaniard. These two saints, so different from each other, were both great masters in their own persons of the grace of abstinence and fasting. Their own personal asceticism was wonderful, and yet these two great lights, though so different from each other, and so mortified themselves, agreed in this—not to impose bodily afflictions to any great extent on their disciples, but mortification of the spirit, of the will, of the affections, of the tastes, of the judgement, of the reason. They were divinely enlightened to see that the coming age, at the beginning of which they stood, required more than anything else, not mortification of the body (though it needed that too, of course,) but more than it mortification of the reason and the will.

Now then I have got at length, my Brethren, to my

practical conclusion. What all of us want more than anything else, what this age wants, is that its intellect and its will should be under a law. At present it is lawless, its will is its own law, its own reason is the standard of all truth. It does not bow to authority, it does not submit to the law of faith. It is wise in its own eyes and it relies on its own resources. And you, as living in the world, are in danger of being seduced by it, and being a partner in its sin, and so coming in at the end for its punishment. Now then let me in conclusion, suggest one or two points in which you may profitably subdue your minds, which require it even more than your bodies.

For example, in respect to curiosity. What a deal of time is lost, to say nothing else, in this day by curiosity, about things which in no ways concern us. I am not speaking against interest in the news of the day altogether, for the course of the world must ever be interesting to a Christian from its bearing upon the fortunes of the Church, but I speak of vain curiosity, love of scandal, love of idle tales, curious prying into the private history of people, curiosity about trials and offences, and personal matters, nay often what is much worse than this, curiosity into sin. What strange diseased curiosity is sometimes felt about the history of murders, and of the malefactors themselves! Worse still, it is shocking to say, but there is so much evil curiosity to know about deeds of darkness, of which the Apostle says that it is shameful to speak. Many a person, who has no intention of doing the like, from an evil curiosity reads what he ought not to read. This is in one shape or other very much the sin of boys, and they suffer for it. The knowledge of what is evil is the first step in their case to the commission of it. Hence this is the way in which we are called upon, with this Lent we now begin, to mortify ourselves. Let us mortify our curiosity.

Again, the desire of knowledge is in itself praiseworthy, but it may be excessive, it may take us from higher things, it may take up too much of our time—it is a vanity. The Preacher makes the distinction between profitable and unprofitable learning when he says, "The words of the wise are like goads and nails." They excite and stimulate us and are fixed in our memories. "But further than this, my son, inquire not. Of making many books there is no end, and much study" (that is, poring over secular subjects,) "is affliction of the flesh. Let us one and all have an end of the discourse: fear God and keep His commandments, for this is the whole of man." Knowledge is very well in its place, but it is like flowers without fruit. We cannot feed on knowledge, we cannot thrive on knowledge. Just as the leaves of the grove are very beautiful but would make a bad meal, so we shall ever be hungry and never be satisfied if we think to take knowledge for our food. Knowledge is no food. Religion is our only food.

Here then is another mortification. Mortify your desire of knowledge. Do not go into excess in seeking after truths which are not religious.

Again, mortify your reason. In order to try you, God puts before you things which are difficult to believe. St. Thomas's faith was tried; so is yours. He said "My Lord and My God." You say so too. Bring your proud intellect into subjection. Believe what you cannot see, what you cannot understand, what you cannot explain, what you cannot prove, when God says it.

Lastly, bring your will into subjection. We all like our own will—let us consult the will of others. Numbers of persons are obliged to do this. Servants are obliged to do the will of their masters, workmen of their employers, children of their parents, husbands of their wives. Well, in these cases let your will go with that of those who have a right to command you. Don't rebel against it. Sanctify what is after all a necessary act. Make it in a certain sense your own, sanctify it, and get merit from it. And again when you are your own master, be on your guard against going too much by your own opinion. Take some wise counsellor or director, and obey him. There are persons who cry out against such obedience, and call it a number of bad names. They are the very persons who need it. It would do them much good. They say that men are made mere machines, and lose the dignity of human nature by going by the word of another. And I should like to know what they become by going by their own will. I appeal to any candid person and ask whether he would not confess that on the whole the world would be much happier, that individuals would be much happier, if they had not a will of their own. For one person who has been hurt by following the direction of another, a hundred persons have been ruined by going by their own will. This is another subject. But this is enough. May almighty God enable you, etc.

THE WORLD AND SIN

Second Sunday in Lent,
19th March, 1848

I**N THE PASSAGE** of St. Matthew's Gospel, part of which is read as the Gospel for this day, we have a very remarkable contrast, the contrast between this world and the unseen world. It is so distinctly drawn out, and so impressive, that it may be profitable to us, with God's grace, to attempt to enlarge upon it.

Our Lord often passed the night in prayer, and, as afterwards in that sad night before His passion He took with Him three apostles to witness His prayer in agony, so at an earlier time, He took the same favoured three with Him to witness His prayer in ecstasy and glory. On the one occasion He fell on His face and prayed more earnestly till He was covered with a sweat of blood which rolled down upon the cold earth. In the other, as He prayed his countenance became bright and glorious, and He was lifted off the earth. So He remained communing with His Father, ministered to by Moses and Elias, till a voice came from the cloud, which said, "This is My beloved Son, hear ye Him." The sight had been so wonderful, so transporting, that St. Peter could not help crying out. He knew not what he said. He did not know how to express his inward feelings, nor did he understand in a moment all the wonders about him. He could but say, "Lord it is good for us to be here." Simple words, but how much they contain in them. It was good, it was the good of man, it was the great good, it was our good. He did not say that the sight was sublime and marvellous. He was not able to reflect upon it and describe it. His reason did not speak, but his affections. He did but say that it was good to be there. And he wished that great good to continue to him ever. He said "Let us build three tabernacles, one for Thee, one for Moses, and one for Elias." He wished to remain there for ever, it was so good. He was loath the vision should come to an end. He did not like to descend from the mount, and return to those whom he had left behind.

Now let us see what was taking place below, while they were above. When they reached the crowd, they found a dispute going on between the rest of the apostles and the Scribes. The subject of it seems to have been the poor demoniac, who is next spoken of. A father had brought his son to be cured by the apostles. He was a frightful maniac, possessed by the devil. None could hold him. The spirit took away his voice and hearing. He was ordinarily deaf and dumb, but sometimes he dashed himself to the ground, threw himself into the fire or into the water, foamed at the mouth, and then perhaps collapsed. The devil was too much for the apostles. They could not master him, they could not cast him out. They were reduced to a sort of despair, and this was the occasion, as it appears, of their dispute with the Scribes, who might be taunting them with their failure. O the contrast between what St. Peter had come from, and what he had now come to! He had left peace, stillness, contemplation, the vision of heaven, and he had come into pain, grief, confusion, perplexity, disappointment, and debate.

Now this contrast, as I have said, between the Mount of Transfiguration and the scene at its foot, fitly represents to us the contrast between the world and the Church, between the things seen and the things unseen.

I will not dwell on the mere physical evils of this life, though they are enough to appal us, the miseries of sickness, pain, want, cold, hunger; but let us dwell upon the moral evils which it contains. The poor youth who was brought to Christ to be cured, was possessed by the devil, and alas! is not a great portion, is not the greatest portion of mankind at this day possessed by the devil too? He is called in Scripture "the god of this world," and "the Prince of the powers of this air, the spirit which now worketh in the children of disbelief." In the book of Job we read of his "compassing the earth and walking up and down in it," and St. Peter speaks of our "adversary the devil, as a roaring lion, compassing the earth, seeking whom he may devour." Thus he is found all over the earth, and within the souls of men, not indeed able to do anything which God does not permit, but still, God not interfering, he possesses immense power, and is able to influence millions upon millions to their ruin. And as the poor epileptic in the gospel was under the mastery of the evil spirit, so that his eyes, his ears, his tongue, his limbs were not his own, so does that same miserable spirit possess the souls of sinners, ruling them, impelling them here and there, doing what he will with them, not indeed doing the same with every one, some he moves one way, some in another, but all in some pitiable, horrible, and ungodly way.

Wickedness is sometimes called madness in Scripture—so it is. As literal madness is derangement of the reason, so sin is derangement of the heart, of the spirit, of the affection. And as madness was the disorder in which possession by the devil showed itself in Scripture, so this madness of the heart and spirit is the disorder which in all ages the devil produces in the spirit. And as there are different forms of that madness which is derangement of the reason, so there are different forms of that worse madness which is sin. In an asylum there are different forms of the disorder, and so this whole world is one vast madhouse, of which the inmates, though shrewd enough in matters of this world, yet in spiritual matters are in one way or another mad.

For example, what is the drunkard but a sort of madman? Who is possessed and ruled by an evil spirit, if not he? He has delivered himself over to the power of Satan, and he is his slave. He cannot do what he would. Through his own fault he cannot do what he would. In that he differs from the real madman, whose fault it is not that he is mad; whereas it is the drunkard's own fault that he is the slave of evil. But so it is, he has put himself under the power of evil, he puts himself away from grace, he cannot make up his mind to will to be otherwise, his will is set on what is evil, and thus he is a mere slave. The relentless spirit of evil carries him off to the haunts of intemperance. He knows that he is ruining himself, soul and body, he knows the misery he brings his family, he knows that he is shortening his life, he curses perhaps his own infatuation while he persists in it. He wishes he had never been born. Perhaps he has a bad illness in consequence, and the medical man who attends him, says to him, that it will to a certainty be his death, if he does not reform. He knows it, yet his sin is too strong for him, and in this despair and agony of mind perhaps he takes up some dreadful belief, most injurious to God's honour and glory, as if he were fated to all this, and could not help it. He says, "Every man is fated to be what he is, it can't be helped, it's not my fault, I never could have been otherwise, it did not depend on me." Miserable and most untrue saying. Is it not the saying of a madman? Is it not the word of one possessed with a devil? Here then is one instance in which the demoniac in the gospel may be taken as a type and emblem of the state of the world.

Others are possessed by spirits of a different kind. They are not outrageous, but they are bowed down to the earth, and kept in a close awful captivity. How many, for instance, are there with hard hearts! And what is hardness of heart but a sort of possession by the evil one? The drunkard has often moments of religious feeling, but there are numbers, and they perhaps what the world calls moral, well conditioned men, who seem to have no heart whatever for spiritual subjects. A true Christian cannot hear the name of Christ without emotion, but in this country there are multitudes, poor and rich, who are set upon nothing else whatever but on getting money, and who have no taste whatever for religion. Sometimes, I say, they are poor, and thus they not merely aim to get a livelihood, for this is right, but are engrossed with the thought. Religion seems to them, not a real thing, but a name, and to concern them no more than what is going on in China or Patagonia. It seems beside the mark, and they merely wonder and stare at those who introduce it. The rich again are engrossed with the wish to make their wealth greater, and the pursuit of wealth blocks up the avenues to their hearts, and they have neither time, nor thought, nor love for the great things which concern their peace. What is all this but another possession of the devil, though very different from the former? It is like moping melancholy. The demoniac in the gospel, not only cried out and tore himself, but at other times he became dry or shrivelled, which seems to mean a sort of collapse. What is this love of the world, which we see whether in rich or poor, but a sort of shrivelling up or collapse of the soul? What then is so like a possession of Satan? And can any state be more fearful than that of an immortal being, who is to live for ever, attempting to live on mortal food, and having no relish for that immortal food, which alone is its true nourishment? 'What is to be your food, my Brethren, when you get into the next world? Will this mortal food on which you feed now, be present to you then? What are your souls then to feed on? What is to employ them? Nay, what is to possess them? If a soul goes on contentedly, now the slave of the evil one, if he lets the evil one take up a lodgement in his breast, how is he to dislodge him ever? Will not that evil spirit necessarily and inevitably carry down that soul at once to hell, when death comes?

I might go on upon this subject at great length, were it necessary. Accustom yourself to the idea, my Brethren, and a terrible idea it is, that the state of sin is a demoniacal possession. Consider how such a possession of the body is spoken of in Scripture. Consider how the devil tormented the poor suffering body which he was allowed to get hold of. Then consider, what we may so often see now, what a fearful affliction madness is. Then, when you have considered these two things, and got a clear hold of the idea, think that sin is just such a possession of the heart and spirit. It is not that the body is afflicted, as in the case of a demoniac. It is not that the reason is afflicted, as in the case of a madman. But it is that the spirit, the heart, the affections, the conscience, the will, are in the power of an evil spirit, who sways them about at his pleasure. How awful is this!

When then St. Peter, St. James, and St. John came down from the Mount, and saw the miserable youth tormented by an evil spirit, they saw in that youth a figure and emblem of that world of sinners, to whom in due time they were to be sent to preach. But this is not all. They found their brethren disputing with the Scribes, or at least the Scribes questioning with them. Here is another circumstance in which the scene which they saw resembled the world. The world is full of wrangling and debate, and not unreasonably, because when the heart is wrong, the reason goes wrong too, and when men corrupt themselves and lead bad lives, then they do not see the truth, but have to hunt about after it, and this creates a great confusion. For instance, suppose a sudden darkness were to fall upon the streets of a crowded city in day time, you may fancy without my telling you what a noise and clamour there would be, foot passengers, carriages, carts, horses all being mixed together. Such is the state of the world. The evil spirit, which worketh in the children of disbelief, the god of this world, as St. Paul says, has blinded the eyes of them that believe not, and hence they are obliged to wrangle and debate, for they have lost their way; and they fall out with each other and one says this and one says that, because they do not see. When men do not *see*, they begin to *reason*. When men do not see, they begin to talk loud. When men do not see, they begin to quarrel. Look around, my Brethren, is it not so? Have not you theories innumerable, arguments interminable offered to you, on all sides? One man says truth is here, another there. Alas, alas, how many religions are there in this great yet unhappy country! Here you have the Scribes wrangling with each other. There is no end of religions—there are new ones continually. Now if one is true, the other is false; if the new is true, the old are false, if the old are true, the new are false. All cannot be true. Can even a dozen be true, or six, or two? Can more than *one* be true? And which is that one? Thank God, we, my Brethren, know which that one is—that is the true religion which has been from the beginning and has been always the same. But on all sides there are wranglings and doubtings and disputings, uncertainty and change.

Now I will mention one other respect in which the scene before the three Apostles when they came down from the mount resembled the world, and that is a still more miserable one. You will observe that their brethren could not cast the evil spirit out. So it is now. There is an immense weight of evil in the world. We Catholics, and especially we Catholic priests, have it in charge to resist, to overcome the evil; but we cannot do what we would, we cannot overcome the giant, we cannot bind the strong man. We do a part of the work, not all. It is a battle which goes on between good and evil, and though by God's grace we do something, we cannot do more. There is confusion of nations and perplexity. It is God's will that so it should be, to show His power. He alone can heal the soul, He alone can expel the devil. And therefore we must wait for a great deal, till He comes down, till He comes down from His seat on high, His seat in glory, to aid us and deliver us.

In that day we shall enter, if we be worthy, the fulness of that glory, of which the three Apostles had the foretaste in the moment of Transfiguration. All is darkness here, all is bright in heaven. All is disorder here, all is order there.

All is noise here, and there there is stillness, or if sounds are heard, they are the sweet sounds of the eternal harps on which the praises of God are sung. Here we are in a state of uncertainty: we do not know what is to happen. The Church suffers; her goodly portion, and her choice inheritance suffer; the vineyard is laid waste; there is persecution and war; and Satan rages and afflicts when he cannot destroy. But all this will be set right in the world to come, and if St. Peter could say at the Transfiguration "It is good to be here," much more shall we have cause to say so when we see the face of God. For then we shall be like our Lord Himself, we shall have glorified bodies, as He had then, and has now. We shall have put off flesh and blood, and receive our bodies at the last day, the same indeed, but incorruptible, spiritual bodies, which will be able to see and enjoy the presence of God in a way which was beyond the three Apostles in the days of their mortality. Then the envious malignant spirit will be cast out, and we shall have nothing to fear, nothing to be perplexed at, for the Lord God shall lighten us, and encompass us, and we shall be in perfect security and peace. Then we shall look back upon this world, and the trials, and temptations which are past, and what thankfulness, what joy will not rise within us—and we shall look forward; and this one thought will be upon us that this blessedness is to last for ever. Our security has no limit. It is not that we shall be promised a hundred years of peace, or a thousand, but for ever and ever shall we be as we are, for our happiness and our peace will be founded in the infinite blessedness and peace of God, and as He is eternal and happy, so shall we be.

May this be the future portion of you all, my Brethren, and in order to that future bliss may the present blessing of God, the Father, etc.

OUR LADY IN THE GOSPEL

Third Sunday in Lent,
26th March, 1848

THERE IS a passage in the Gospel of this day, which may have struck many of us as needing some illustration. While our Lord was preaching, a woman in the crowd cried out, "Blessed is the womb that bore Thee and the breasts which Thou hast sucked" (Luke 11:27). Our Lord assents, but instead of dwelling on the good words of this woman, He goes on to say something further. He speaks of a greater blessedness. "Yea," He says, "but blessed are they who hear the word of God and keep it." Now these words of our Lord require notice, if it were only for this reason, because there are many persons nowadays who think they are said in depreciation of the glory and blessedness of the Most Holy Virgin Mary; as if our Lord had said, "My Mother is blessed, but my true servants are more blessed than she is." I shall say some words then on this passage, and with a peculiar fitness, because we have just passed the festival of Lady Day, the great feast on which we commemorate the Annunciation, that is, the visit of the Angel Gabriel to her, and the miraculous conception of the Son of God, her Lord and Saviour, in her womb.

Now a very few words will be sufficient to show that our Lord's words are no disparagement to the dignity and glory of His Mother, as the first of creatures and the Queen of all Saints. For consider, He says that it is a more blessed thing to keep His commandments than to be His Mother, and do you think that the Most Holy Mother of God did not keep the commandments of God? Of course no one, no Protestant even—no one will deny she did. Well, if so, what our Lord says is that the Blessed Virgin was *more* blessed in that she kept His commandments than because she was His Mother. And what Catholic denies this? On the contrary we all confess it. All Catholics confess it. The Holy Fathers of the Church tell us again and again that our Lady was more blessed in doing God's will than in being His Mother. She was blessed in two ways. She was blessed in being His Mother; she was blessed in being filled with the spirit of faith and obedience. And the latter blessedness was the greater. I say the Holy Fathers say so expressly. St. Augustine says, "More blessed was Mary in receiving the faith of Christ, than in receiving the flesh of Christ." In like manner St. Elizabeth says to her at the Visitation, "*Beata es quae credidisti*, Blessed art thou who didst believe"; and St. Chrysostom goes so far as to say that she would not have been blessed, even though she had borne Christ in the body, unless she had heard the word of God and kept it.

Now I have used the expression "St. Chrysostom goes *so far* as to say," not that it is not a plain truth. I say, it is a plain truth that the Blessed Virgin would not have been blessed, though she had been the Mother of God, if she had not done His will, but it is an extreme thing to say, for it is supposing a thing impossible, it is supposing that she could be so highly favoured and yet not be inhabited and possessed by God's grace, whereas the Angel, when he came, expressly hailed her as full of grace. "*Ave, gratia plena.*" The two blessednesses cannot be divided. (Still it is remarkable that she herself had an opportunity of contrasting and dividing them, and that she preferred to keep God's commandments to being His Mother, if she could not have both.) She who was chosen to be the Mother of God was also chosen to be *gratia plena*, full of grace. This you see is an explanation of those high doctrines which are received among Catholics concerning the purity and sinlessness of the Blessed Virgin. St. Augustine will not listen to the notion that she ever committed sin, and the Holy Council of Trent declares that by special privilege she through all her life avoided all, even venial sin. And at this time you know it is the received belief of Catholics that she was not conceived in original sin, and that her conception was immaculate.

Whence come these doctrines? They come from the great principle contained in our Lord's words on which I am commenting. He says, "More blessed is it to do God's will than to be God's Mother." Do not say that Catholics do not feel this deeply—so deeply do they feel it that they are ever enlarging on her virginity, purity, immaculateness, faith, humility and obedience. Never say then that Catholics forget this passage of Scripture. Whenever they keep the Feast of the Immaculate Conception, the Purity, or the like, recollect it is because they make so much of the blessedness of sanctity. The woman in the crowd cried out, "Blessed is the womb and the breasts of Mary." She spoke in faith; she did not mean to exclude her higher blessedness, but her words only went a certain way. Therefore our Lord completed them. And therefore His Church after Him, dwelling on the great and sacred mystery of His Incarnation, has ever felt that she, who so immediately ministered to it, must have been most holy. And therefore for the honour of the Son she has ever extolled the glory of the Mother. As we give Him of our best, ascribe to Him what is best, as on earth we make our churches costly and beautiful; as when He was taken down from the cross,

His pious servants wrapped Him in fine linen, and laid Him in a tomb in which never man was laid; as His dwelling place in heaven is pure and stainless—so much more ought to be—so much more was—that tabernacle from which He took flesh, in which He lay, holy and immaculate and divine. As a body was prepared for Him, so was the place of that body prepared also. Before the Blessed Mary could be Mother of God, and in order to her being Mother, she was set apart, sanctified, filled with grace, and made meet for the presence of the Eternal.

And the Holy Fathers have ever gathered the exact obedience and the sinlessness of the Blessed Virgin from the very narrative of the Annunciation, when she became the Mother of God. For when the Angel appeared to her and declared to her the will of God, they say that she displayed especially four graces, humility, faith, obedience and purity. Nay, these graces were as it were, preparatory conditions to her being made the minister of so high a dispensation. So that if she had not had faith, and humility, and purity, and obedience, she would not have merited to be God's Mother. Thus it is common to say that she conceived Christ in mind before she conceived Him in body, meaning that the blessedness of faith and obedience preceded the blessedness of being a Virgin Mother. Nay, they even say that God waited for her consent before He came into her and took flesh of her. Just as He did no mighty works in one place because they had not faith, so this great miracle, by which He became the Son of a creature, was suspended till she was tried and found meet for it—till she obeyed.

But there is something more to be added to this. I said just now that the two blessednesses could not be divided, that they went together. "Blessed is the womb," etc.; "Yea, rather blessed," etc. It is true, but observe this. The Holy Fathers always teach that in the Annunciation, when the Angel appeared to our Lady, she showed that she preferred what our Lord called the greater of the two blessednesses to the other. For when the Angel announced to her that she was destined to have that blessedness which Jewish women had age after age looked out for, to be the Mother of the expected Christ, she did not seize the news, as another would, but she waited. She waited till she could be told it was consistent with her Virgin state. She was unwilling to accept this most wonderful honour, unwilling till she could be satisfied on this point. "How shall this be, since I know not man?" They consider that she had made a vow of virginity, and considered that holy estate a greater thing than to bear the Christ. Such is the teaching of the Church, showing distinctly how closely she observes the doctrine of the words of Scripture on which I am commenting, how intimately she considers that the Blessed Mary felt them, viz. that though blessed was the womb that bore Christ and the breasts which He sucked, yet more blessed was the soul which owned that womb and those breasts, more blessed was the soul full of grace, which because it was so gracious was rewarded with the extraordinary privilege to be made the Mother of God.

But now a further question arises, which it may be worth considering. It may be asked, Why did our blessed Lord even *seem* to extenuate the honour and privilege of His Mother? When the woman said, "Blessed is the womb," etc., He answered indeed, "*Yea*." But He went on, "Yea, rather blessed." And on another occasion, if not on this, He said when someone told Him that His Mother and brethren were without, "Who is My Mother?" etc. And at an earlier time, when He began His miracles, and His Mother told Him that the guests in the marriage feast had no wine, He said, "Woman, what have I to do with thee? Mine hour is not yet come." These passages seem to be coldly worded towards the Blessed Virgin, even though the sense may be satisfactorily explained. What then do they mean? Why did He so speak?

Now I shall give two reasons in explanation:

1. The first which more immediately rises out of what I have been saying is this: that for many centuries the Jewish women had looked out each of them to be the Mother of the expected Christ, and had not associated it apparently with any higher sanctity. Therefore they had been so

desirous of marriage; therefore marriage was held in such special honour by them. Now marriage is an ordinance of God, and Christ has made it a sacrament—yet there is a higher state, and that the Jews did not understand. Their whole idea was to associate religion with pleasures of this world. They did not know, commonly speaking, what it was to give up this world for the next. They did not understand that poverty was better than riches, ill name than good name, fast and abstinence than feasting, and virginity than marriage. And therefore when the woman in the crowd cried out upon the blessedness of the womb that bore Him and the breasts that He had sucked, He taught her and all who heard Him that the soul was greater than the body, and that to be united to Him in spirit was more than to be united to Him in flesh.

2. This is one reason, and the other is more interesting to us. You know that our Saviour for the first thirty years of His earthly life lived under the same roof as His Mother. When He returned from Jerusalem at the age of twelve with her and St. Joseph, it is expressly said that He was subject to them. This is a very strong expression, but that subjection, that familiar family life, was not to last to the end. Even on the occasion upon which the Evangelist says that He was subject to them, He had said and done what emphatically conveyed to them that He had other duties. For He had left them and stayed in the Temple

among the doctors, and when they expressed surprise, He answered, "Wist ye not that I ought to be in the things which are My Father's?" This was, I say, an anticipation of the time of His Ministry, when He was to leave His home. For thirty years He remained there, but, as He was steadily observant of His home duties, while they were His duties, so was He zealous about His Father's work, when the time came for His performing it. When the time of His mission came, He left His home and His Mother and, dear as she was to Him, He put her aside.

In the Old Testament the Levites are praised because they knew not father or mother, when duty to God came in the way. "Who said to his father and to his mother, I know you not, and to his brothers, I am ignorant of you" (Deut 33:9). "They knew not their children." If such was the conduct of the sacerdotal tribe under the Law, well did it become the great and one Priest of the New Covenant to give a pattern of that virtue which was found and rewarded in Levi. He too Himself has said, "He who loveth father or mother more than Me, is not worthy of Me." And He tells us that "every one who hath left home or brothers or sisters or father or mother or wife or children or lands for His name's sake, shall receive a hundredfold and shall possess eternal life" (Matt 19:29). It became then Him who gave the precept to set the example, and as He told his followers to leave all they had for the Kingdom's sake, *in His own Person* to do all that He could, to leave all He had, to leave His home and His Mother, when He had to preach the Gospel.

Therefore it was that from the beginning of His ministry, He gave up His Mother. At the time He did His first miracle, He proclaimed it. He did that miracle at her bidding, but He implied, or rather declared, that He was then beginning to separate from her. He said, "What is between Me and thee?" And again, "My hour is not yet come," that is, The hour cometh when I shall acknowledge thee again, 0 my Mother. The hour cometh when thou rightly and powerfully wilt intercede with Me. The hour cometh when at thy bidding I will do miracles: it cometh, but it is not yet come. And till it is come "What is between thee and Me? I know thee not. For the time I have forgotten thee."

From that time we have no record of His seeing His Mother till He saw her under His Cross. He parted with her. Once she tried to see Him. A report went about that He was beside Himself. His friends went out to get possession of Him. The Blessed Virgin apparently did not like to be left behind. She went Out too. A message came to Him that they were seeking Him, could not reach Him for the press. Then He said those serious words, "Who is My Mother?" etc., meaning, as it would appear, that He had left all for God's service, and that, as for our sake He had been born of the Virgin, so for our sake He gave up His Virgin Mother, that He might glorify His heavenly Father and do His work.

Such was His separation from the Blessed Mary, but when on the Cross He said, "It is finished," this time of separation was at an end. And therefore before it His blessed Mother had joined Him, and He seeing her, recognized her again. His hour was come, and He said to her of St. John, "Woman, behold thy son," and to St. John, "Behold thy Mother."

And now, my Brethren, in conclusion I will but say one thing. I do not wish your words to outrun your real feeling. I do not wish you to take up books containing the praises of the Ever Blessed Virgin, and to use them and imitate them rashly without consideration. But be sure of this, that if you cannot enter into the warmth of foreign books of devotion, it is a deficiency in you. To use strong words will not mend the matter; it is a fault within which can only gradually be overcome, but it is a deficiency, for this reason, if for no other. Depend upon it, the way to enter into the sufferings of the Son, is to enter into the sufferings of the Mother. Place yourselves at the foot of the Cross, see Mary standing there, looking up and pierced with the sword. Imagine her feelings, make them your own. Let her be your great pattern. Feel what she felt and you will worthily mourn over the death and passion of your and her Saviour. Have her simple faith, and you will believe well. Pray to be filled with the grace given to her. Alas, you must have many feelings she had not, the feeling of personal sin, of personal sorrow, of contrition, and self hate, but these will in a sinner naturally accompany the faith, the humility, the simplicity which were her great ornaments. Lament with her, believe with her, and at length you will experience her blessedness of which the text speaks. None indeed can have her special prerogative, and be the Mother of the Highest, but you will have a share in that blessedness of hers which is greater, the blessedness of doing God's will and keeping His commandments.

STEWARDS AND ALSO SONS OF GOD

*Eigth Sunday after Pentecost,
31st July, 1870*

HE Parable of the Unjust Steward which is the subject of today's Gospel is more difficult to understand than most of our Lord's Parables—but there are some points in its teaching which it is impossible to mistake.

First in its literal sense it presents us with a view of human society, as it is, which is true in all ages, now as much as when our Lord spoke. Nothing is more common now in the world than that sort of dishonesty which is instanced in the Unjust Steward. He was in trust with his master's property; he treated it as if it were his own; he wasted it either by carelessness or by spending it on himself. He forgot his duty to his employer, as men do now, and as men now borrow money without rational expectations of repaying it, and thus involve themselves and are unable to meet the claims made on them. Such was the case of the Steward: he was called upon to make his account good, and he could not do so. Under these circumstances he was led on to commit a second sin in order to conceal the first. He took his master's creditors into his counsel, and formed with them a plan of fraudulent returns with the purpose of making his books right. This, I say, is the first picture presented to us in this Parable, and it impresses on us by an instance St. Paul's warning, "The love of money is the root of all evil."

But a larger sense of the Parable, and one on which I shall rather insist is this: the view which it gives us of our duties to God and our conduct under those duties. It is plain that the Master spoken of by our Lord is Almighty God Himself; and by the Steward is meant each of His creatures, His rational creatures, who have goods, or, as is sometimes said, talents committed to them, by Him. He does not give these goods to us, but He lends them to us in order that we return them to Him, when our time is ended, with fruit or interest. Men in trade by means of money make money; and as at the end of a certain time capital is thus increased, so by using God's gifts well during the years of this mortal life, we are able to render in to Him a good account and return His gifts with interest. This is the meaning of the Parable of the Talents.

And so as regards the Parable of the Steward, on

which I am now remarking, fields and market-gardens and woods yield a produce, and are the means of wealth; such are hay, wheat and other kinds of corn, and various fruits and vegetables in this country; such are olive yards, vine-yards, sugar canes, and other produce of the land abroad. As then money creates money, as the land bears bread, wine and oil, so our souls should yield the due return to God for the many gifts which He has bestowed upon us.

I am speaking of those gifts which belong to our nature, our birth, or our circumstances; gifts of this world. He has given us the means of worshipping Him and doing Him service. He has given us reason, and a certain measure of abilities, more or less. He has given us health, more or less. He has placed us in a certain station of life, high or low. He has given us a certain power of influencing others. He has given us a certain circle of persons, larger or smaller, who depend on us, whom our words and our actions affect for good or for evil, and ought to affect for good. He has given us our share of opportunities of doing good to others. All these are God's gifts to us, and they are given us, not to be wasted, but to be used, to be turned to account. The Steward in the Parable wasted them; and was made responsible for his waste. And so in our own case, we may waste them, as most men waste them; nay worse, we may not only squander them away, we do not know how; but we may actually misapply them, we may use them actually to the injury of Him who has given them to us; but whether we do nothing with them for God, or actually go on to use them to His dishonour and against the interests of truth and religion, (and the latter is more likely than the former, for not to do good with them is in fact to do evil,) anyhow we shall have one day to answer for our use of them.

Thus the Parable before us applies to all of us, as having certain goods committed to us by our Divine Master with a day of reckoning for them in prospect. But this is not all. Charges were brought against the Steward, and his employer called on him to answer them, or rather examined them, and found them well-founded. And so it is sometimes with us, that our conscience, which is the voice of God in the soul, upbraids us, brings before us our neglect of duty, the careless, the irreligious, the evil life which we are leading, our disregard of God's commands, glory, and worship; and anticipates that judgement which is to come. Now sometimes this self-accusation leads us to true repentance and change of life—certainly, praise be to God, this is sometimes the case; but more frequently, instead of turning us into the right path, it has the effect of making us go more wrong than we were before. When the Steward found he could not make good what his Lord had a right to demand of him, he had three courses before him besides that which he adopted; he might have made his debts good by extra work; again he might have got friends to have supplied the deficiency; or, he might have thrown himself on his Lord's mercy. He might have digged, or he might have begged; but he rejected both means. "I cannot dig," he said, "to beg I am ashamed." So he went off into a further act of dishonesty to the disadvantage of his master. And in like manner, we, when we have been unfaithful to our good God and feel compunction for that unfaithfulness, have two modes of recovery: we might dig, that is, we might do works of penance; we might vigorously change our life; we might fight with our bad habits; we might redeem the time; that is, we might dig. But we cannot make up our minds to this laborious course; it is too great a sacrifice; it is above us; we cannot dig. And secondly we might beg; that is, we might pray God to forgive us and to change us; we might go to confess our sin and beg for absolution; we might beg the prayers of others, the prayers of the Saints; but to many men, especially to those who are not Catholics, this is more difficult even than labour: "to beg we are ashamed." Begging seems something inconsistent with what they call the dignity of human nature; they think it unmanly, cowardly, slavish; it wounds their pride to confess themselves miserable sinners, to come to a priest, to say the Rosary, to give themselves to certain devotions, day after day; they think such a course as much beneath them as a valiant effort to overcome themselves is above them. They cannot dig, to beg they are ashamed; and therefore they attempt to destroy the sense of their sins, which has fallen upon them by some means worse than those sins themselves—I mean, such as denying perhaps that there is any such thing as sin, saying that it is a bugbear invented by priests, nay perhaps going so far as to say that there is no judgement to come, no God above who will see and will judge what they say or do.

Such is the repentance of men of the world, when conscience reproaches them. It is not a true turning from sin, but a turning to worse sin—they go on to *deny* the Holy Commandment because they have *transgressed* it; they explain away the sinfulness of sin because they have sinned. St. Paul speaks of this evil repentance, if it may be called by that name, in his Second Epistle to the Corinthians, when he says to them the words of 2 Cor. vii. 10. Such is the state of mankind as we see it realized on a large scale on the face of human society in the world at large. When they do evil, act against their conscience and clear duty, there is this opposition between what they know and what they do; light becomes darkness, and instead of the light within them destroying their tendencies to sin, their sins dim or stifle that light, and they become worse than they were, because they were bad already.

This lesson I draw from today's Gospel. Now let us turn to today's Epistle, which carries on the lesson farther, and that both for our warning, and for our encouragement and comfort. It is taken from St. Paul's Epistle to the Romans, and begins thus: "Brethren: We are debtors, not to the flesh, to live according to the flesh; for if you live according to the flesh, you shall die." Now here first we must see what is the meaning of the flesh. At first sight it may seem to mean human nature, but that is not its exact meaning. To explain it, I will turn to the 40th chapter of Isaias. In it is the great promise of the coming of Christ, the preaching of His forerunner, St. John Baptist, and the gifts of the Gospel. The Prophet begins, "Be comforted, be comforted, my people," and he speaks of the voice crying in the wilderness ... Then he says, (which is the passage to which I especially refer), "All flesh is grass, and its goodness is like the flower of the field ... " Now is not the grass, and are not the flowers of the field in themselves good? Does not our Lord say that they are more beautiful than Solomon in all his glory? Certainly. But what is their defect? They fade—our Lord says that today they are and tomorrow are cast into the oven. That is the case with the human soul. Of course it cannot die as the flowers of the field; but its first estate dies. Whatever there is of good in it, whatever of virtue, dies out of the soul as life goes on, as the flowers die, as the human body dies; and as the flowers are at length (as our Lord says) cast into the oven, as fuel, fair as they once were, so much more does the moral excellence of man die, as time goes on; and the longer he lives, the harder, the colder, the uglier in God's sight, the deader, I may say, he becomes.

Now we shall see what St. Paul's meaning is. When he speaks of the flesh, he means human nature in its state of decay, in that state into which he is sure to fall, as times goes on; and he says, "If ye live according to the flesh, ye shall die." If, like the Unjust Steward, we live in the mere way of nature, we shall soon lose all the little good that nature has on starting; and become worse and worse, as time goes on, just as the Steward went from one sin to another, till we reach a state of spiritual death. For all flesh is grass; and this is the beginning and end of the matter; this is the end of all our hopes, all our aspirations, as far as nature is concerned—utter, desperate ruin.

And now I come to the light which dawns upon this darkness, the light which rises over against it, illuminating this solemn history; a light by which a lesson which is so painful, so depressing, becomes a consolation and an encouragement. Blessed be God, that though such is the state of nature, God has not left us in a mere state of nature, but has come to our relief, and brought us into a state higher than our own nature, and thereby destroyed this tangle, this web, this bond, in which mankind lies. He has sent to us

His dearly beloved Son, Jesus Christ, to give us the gifts of grace, which is a divine power above nature, or what is called supernatural, by which we are able to do what nature of itself cannot do. Isaias says, "All flesh is grass"; but St. Peter in his first Epistle (1 Pet 1:24) takes up the word, draws out the happy contrast between nature and grace, and reminds us that by means of the power of grace, what was flesh is flesh no longer, but is spirit; that is, the grace of the Holy Ghost changes our hearts, according to our Lord's words in St. John, "that which is born of the flesh is flesh, but that which is born of the Spirit is spirit."

This great and blessed announcement is made again and again in the New Testament by our Lord and His Apostles; but let me confine myself to what is told us in the Epistle for this day. St. Paul says, "Brethren: we are debtors, not to the flesh, to live according to the flesh." That is, we owe nothing to the flesh. What has the flesh done for us? It is nothing else than the corruption of our nature; the flesh is pride, wrath, hatred, malice, impurity, intemperance, craft, guile; or as St. Paul expressly says himself to the Galatians: "The works of the flesh are manifest, which are ..." (Gal 5:19). What then do we owe to the flesh? We owe sin, misery, a bad conscience, displeasure, spiritual death, future punishment. It has done nothing good for us, and cannot—"for if (he continues) you live according to the flesh, you shall die"; and after saying this, he goes on in wonderful words to enlarge on the contrast of our state, if we have, and if we profit by, the gift of the Spirit.

It is by this gift of the Spirit, that is, by the unmerited supernatural grace of God, that we are set free from that law of sin and death, the law of the flesh, which is the state in which we are born. That tangle of the mind by which our best faculties are kept from rising to Almighty God and seeking their true end and doing their duty, and growing in all good, is a bondage, a slavery, and the grace of God sets us free of it, so that we may (as it were) rise on our feet, and become in St. Peter's words good stewards of the manifold gifts of God. Again this grace not only sets us free, so that instead of being slaves we are able to serve God, but it does something more for us. It would be a great thing, if we were allowed to be faithful servants of God, as the Unjust Steward ought to have been, but grace makes us that and something more; we become not merely servants but even Sons of God. What a second wonderful privilege is this! Though we were slaves of sin and the evil one, He not only sets us free from that slavery, and takes us into His house and His service; but, more than that, He adopts us to be His children. This is a second wonderful gift of grace. But there is a third: sons are heirs of their Father, and in like manner He gives us an inheritance; and an inheritance as far above any thing which our nature, even though it were ever so perfect, could merit, viz., the sight of Him hereafter, and eternal life. As paradise is beyond any thing which our sin could inherit, as sin never can merit God's mercy, but simply merits punishment, so human nature, though ever so pure and perfect, could never merit heaven.

These are the great mercies of God which have reversed the state in which we were born, and enabled us to give a good account of our stewardship. He has fortified nature by means of grace; He has overcome the flesh in us by His supernatural aid, and that by three wonderful gifts: first, He has made us faithful servants, whereas without His aid we can be but Unjust Stewards; secondly He makes us not only faithful servants, but dear sons; and thirdly He not only blesses us in this life, but He promises us life everlasting, according to St. Paul's account in today's Epistle, which I will read again ...

What a view this opens on us both of consolation and of solemn thought! Nothing can harm us, the Sons of God, while we remain in our Father's house. Nothing can deprive us of our hope of heaven. But on the other hand how little we understand our privileges; how little we understand the words of the sacred writers about them. May God enlighten our eyes to see what the privileges are—"that you may know what the hope is of His calling, and what are the riches of the glory of His inheritance in the saints" (Eph 1:18).

THE INFIDELITY OF THE FUTURE

Opening of St. Bernard's Seminary,
2nd October, 1873

T IS NO common occasion of thankfulness to the Giver of all good, the Divine Head of the Church, that has led our Rt. Revd. Father, the Bishop of this Diocese, to call us this morning from our several homes to this place. It is with no common gladness, with no ordinary words of rejoicing and congratulations on their lips, that so many of his priests and of his devout laity have met him here today in consequence of his invitation. At length this Seminary is completed and in occupation, which has been for so long a course of years a vision before his mind, and the subject of his prayers and exertions. Years and years ago I have heard him say, that he never could be at rest, till he was enabled by God's mercy to accomplish this great work, and God has heard his persevering prayers and blessed his unwearied exertions. I might say with truth, that even before some of you, my dear Brethren, were born, or at least from the time that you were in your cradles, he, as the chief Pastor of this diocese, when as yet you knew him not, has been engaged in that great undertaking, of which you, by God's inscrutable grace, enjoy the benefits without your own labours.

It is indeed a great event in this diocese, a great event, I may say, in the history of English Catholics, that at length the injunctions of Ecumenical Councils, the tradition of the Church, the desire of the Sovereign Pontiff, are fulfilled among us, and the Bishop's Throne is erected not merely in a dwelling of brick or stone, in the midst of those in whom Christ is to be formed by his teaching, that they in turn may be the edification and light and strength of the generation which is to come after him.

This handing down of the truth from generation to generation is obviously the direct reason for the institution of seminaries for the education of the clergy. Christianity is one religious idea. Superhuman in its origin, it differs from all other religions. As man differs from quadruped, bird or reptile, so does Christianity differ from the superstitions, heresies, and philosophies which are around it. It has a theology and an ethical system of its own. This is its indestructible idea. How are we to secure and perpetuate in this world that gift from above? How are we to preserve to the Christian people this gift, so special, so divine, so easily hid or lost amid the imposing falsehoods with which the world abounds?

The divine provision is as follows. Each circle of Christians has its own priest, who is the representative of the divine idea to that circle in its theological and ethical aspects. He teaches his people, he catechizes their children, bringing them one and all into that form of doctrine, which is his own. But the Church is made up of *many* such circles. How are we to secure that they may *all* speak one and the same doctrine? and that the doctrine of the Apostles? Thus: by the rule that their respective priests should in their turn all be taught from one and the same centre, viz., their common Father, the Bishop of the diocese. They are educated in one school, that is, in one seminary; under the rule, by the voice and example of him who is the One Pastor of all those collections or circles of Christians, of whom they all in time to come are to be the teachers. Catholic doctrine, Catholic morals, Catholic worship and discipline, the Christian character, life, and conduct, all that is necessary for being a good priest, they learn one and all from this religious school, which is the appointed preparation for the ministerial offices. As youths are prepared for their secular calling by schools and teachers who teach what their calling requires, as there are classical schools, commercial schools, teachers for each profession, teachers of the several arts and sciences, so the sacred ministers of the Church are made true representatives of their Bishop when they are appointed to the charge of the Christian people, because they come from one centre of education and from the tutelage of one head.

Hence it is that St. Ignatius, the Martyr Bishop of Antioch, in the first century of the Church, speaking of the ecclesiastical hierarchy, comparing the union of the sacred orders with the Bishop, likens it to a harp which is in perfect tune. He says in his Epistle to the Ephesians, "It becomes you to concur in the mind of your Bishop, as indeed you do. For your estimable body of clergy, worthy of God, is in exact harmony with your Bishop, as the strings to the harp. Hence it is that in your unanimity and concordant charity Jesus Christ is sung. And one by one you take your parts in the choir, so as to sing with one voice through Jesus Christ to the Father that He may hear your petitions" (*ad Eph.* 4).

And if at all times this simple unity, this perfect understanding of the members with the Head, is necessary for the healthy action of the Church, especially is it necessary in these perilous times. I know that all times are perilous, and that in every time serious and anxious minds, alive to the honour of God and the needs of man, are apt to consider no times so perilous as their own. At all times the enemy of souls assaults with fury the Church which is their true Mother, and at least threatens and frightens when he fails in doing mischief. And all times have their special trials which others have not. And so far I will admit that there were certain specific dangers to Christians at certain other times, which do not exist in this time. Doubtless, but still admitting this, still I think that the trials which lie before us are such as would appal and make dizzy even such courageous hearts as St. Athanasius, St. Gregory I, or St. Gregory VII. And they would confess that dark as the prospect of their own day was to them severally, ours has a darkness different in kind from any that has been before it.

The special peril of the time before us is the spread of that plague of infidelity, that the Apostles and our Lord Himself have predicted as the worst calamity of the last times of the Church. And at least a shadow, a typical image of the last times is coming over the world. I do not mean to presume to say that this is the last time, but that it has had the evil prerogative of being like that more terrible season, when it is said that the elect themselves will be in danger of falling away. This applies to all Christians in the world, but it concerns me at this moment, speaking to you, my dear Brethren, who are being educated for our own priesthood, to see how it is likely to be fulfilled in this country.

1. And first it is obvious that while the various religious bodies and sects which surround us according to

God's permission have done untold harm to the cause of Catholic truth in their opposition to us, they have hitherto been of great service to us in shielding and sheltering us from the assaults of those who believed less than themselves or nothing at all. To take one instance, the approved miracles of the Saints are not more wonderful than the miracles of the Bible. Now the Church of England, the Wesleyans, the Dissenters, nay the Unitarians have defended the miracles of the Bible and thereby have given an indirect protection to the miracles of ecclesiastical history. Nay, some of their divines have maintained certain ecclesiastical miracles, as the appearance of the Cross to Constantine, the subterranean fire in Julian's attempt to build the Jewish Temple, etc. And so again the doctrines of the Holy Trinity, the Incarnation, Atonement, etc., though as strange to the reason as those Catholic doctrines which they reject, have been held by many of these bodies with more or less distinctness, and thereby we have been unassailed when we have taught them. But in these years before us it will be much if those outlying bodies are able to defend their own dogmatic professions. Most of them, nearly all of them, already give signs of the pestilence having appeared among them. And as time goes on, when there will be a crisis and a turning point, with each of them, then it will be found that, instead of their position being in any sense a defence for us, it will be found in possession of the enemy. A remnant indeed may be faithful to their light, as the great Novatian body stood by the Catholics and suffered with them during the Arian troubles, but we shall in vain look for that safeguard from what may be called the orthodoxy of these Protestant communions, which we have hitherto profited by.

2. Again another disadvantage to us will arise from our very growth in numbers and influence in this country. The Catholic Religion, when it has a free course, always must be a power in a country. This is the mere consequence of its divine origin. While Catholics were few and oppressed by disabilities, they were suffered and were at peace. But now that those disabilities are taken off and Catholics are increasing in number, it is impossible that they should not come in collision with the opinions, the prejudices, the objects of a Protestant country, and that without fault on any side, except that the country is Protestant. Neither party will understand the other, and then the old grievances in history which this country has against Rome will be revived and operate to our disadvantage. It is true that this age is far more gentle, kind and generous than former ages, and Englishmen, in their ordinary state, are not cruel, but they may easily be led to believe that their generosity may be abused on our part, that they were unwise in liberating those who are in fact their mortal enemies. And this general feeling of fear of us may be such as, even

with a show of reason, to turn against us even generous minds, so that from no fault of ours, but from the natural antagonism of a religion which cannot change with the new political states into which the whole world is gradually moulding itself, may place us in temporal difficulties, of which at present we have no anticipation.

And it cannot be denied that there is just now threatening the political world such a calamity. There are many influential men who think that things are not indeed ripe as yet for such a measure, but who look forward to the times, when whether the one or the other great political party in the State may make it their cry at the elections of a new Parliament, that they propose to lessen the influence of Catholics and circumscribe their privileges. And however this may be, two things, I think, are plain, that we shall become more and more objects of distrust to the nation at large, and that our Bishops and Priests will be associated in the minds of men with the political acts of foreign Catholics, and be regarded as members of one extended party in all countries, the enemies, as will be thought, of civil liberty and of national progress. In this way we may suffer disadvantages which have not weighed upon the Catholic Church since the age of Constantine.

3. I repeat, when Catholics are a small body in a country, they cannot easily become a mark for their enemies, but our prospect in this time before us is that we shall be

so large that our concerns cannot be hid, and at the same time so unprotected that we cannot but suffer. No large body can be free from scandals from the misconduct of its members. In medieval times the Church had its courts in which it investigated and set right what was wrong, and that without the world knowing much about it. Now the state of things is the very reverse. With a whole population able to read, with cheap newspapers day by day conveying the news of every court, great and small to every home or even cottage, it is plain that we are at the mercy of even one unworthy member or false brother. It is true that the laws of libel are a great protection to us as to others. But the last few years have shown us what harm can be done us by the mere infirmities, not so much as the sins, of one or two weak minds. There is an immense store of curiosity directed upon us in this country, and in great measure an unkind, a malicious curiosity. If there ever was a time when one priest will be a spectacle to men and angels it is in the age now opening upon us.

4. Nor is this all. This general intelligence of every class of society, general but shallow, is the means of circulating all through the population all the misrepresentations which the enemies of the Church make of her faith and her teaching. Most falsehoods have some truth in them; at least those falsehoods which are perversions of the truth are the most successful. Again, when there is no

falsehood, yet you know how strange truth may appear to minds unfamiliar with it. You know that the true religion must be full of mysteries—and therefore to Catholicism, if to any profession, any body of men at all, applies the proverb that a fool may ask a hundred questions which a wise man cannot answer. It is scarcely possible so to answer inquiries or objections on a great number of points of our faith or practice, as to be intelligible or persuasive to them. And hence the popular antipathy to Catholicism seems, and will seem more and more, to be based upon reason, or common sense, so that first the charge will seem to all classes of men true that the Church stifles the reason of man, and next that, since it is impossible for educated men, such as her priests, to believe what is so opposite to reason, they must be hypocrites, professing what in their hearts they reject.

5. I have more to say on this subject. There are, after all, real difficulties in Revealed Religion. There are questions, in answer to which we can only say, "I do not know." There are arguments which cannot be met satisfactorily, from the nature of the case—because our minds, which can easily enough understand the objections, are not in their present state able to receive the true answer. Nay, human language perhaps has not words to express it in. Or again, perhaps the right answer is possible, and is set down in your books of theology, and you know it. But

things look very different in the abstract and the concrete. You come into the world, and fall in with the living objector and inquirer, and your answer you find scattered to the winds. The objection comes to you now with the force of a living expositor of it, recommended by the earnestness and sincerity with which he holds it, with his simple conviction of its strength and accompanied by all the collateral or antecedent probabilities, which he heaps around it. You are not prepared for his objection being part of a system of thought, each part of which bears one way and supports the other parts. And he will appeal to any number of men, friends or others, who agree with him, and they each will appeal to him and all the rest to the effect that the Catholic view and arguments simply cannot be supported. Perhaps the little effect you produce by the arguments which you have been taught is such that you are quite disheartened and despond.

6. I am speaking of evils, which in their intensity and breadth are peculiar to these times. But I have not yet spoken of the root of all these falsehoods—the root as it ever has been, but hidden; but in this age exposed to view and unblushingly avowed—I mean, that spirit of infidelity itself which I began by referring to as the great evil of our times, though of course when I spoke of the practical force of the objections which we constantly hear and shall hear made to Christianity, I showed it is from this spirit

that they gain their plausibility. The elementary proposition of this new philosophy which is now so threatening is this—that in all things we must go by reason, in nothing by faith, that things are known and are to be received so far as they can be proved. Its advocates say, all other knowledge has proof—why should religion be an exception? And the mode of proof is to advance from what we know to what we do not know, from sensible and tangible facts to sound conclusions. The world pursued the way of faith as regards physical nature, and what came of it? Why, that till three hundred years ago they believed, because it was the tradition, that the heavenly bodies were fixed in solid crystalline spheres and moved round the earth in the course of twenty-four hours. Why should not that method which has done so much in physics, avail also as regards that higher knowledge which the world has believed it had gained through revelation? There is no revelation from above. There is no exercise of faith. Seeing and proving is the only ground for believing. They go on to say, that since proof admits of degrees, a demonstration can hardly be had except in mathematics; we never can have simple knowledge; truths are only probably such. So that faith is a mistake in two ways. First, because it usurps the place of reason, and secondly because it implies an absolute assent to doctrines, and is dogmatic, which absolute assent is irrational. Accordingly you will find, certainly in the future, nay more, *even now, even now*, that the writers and thinkers of the day do not even believe there is a God. They do not believe either the *object*—a God personal, a Providence and a moral Governor; and secondly, what they *do* believe, viz., that there is some first cause or other, they do not believe with faith, absolutely, but as a probability.

You will say that their theories have been in the world and are no new thing. No. Individuals have put them forth, but they have not been current and popular ideas. Christianity has never yet had experience of a world simply irreligious. Perhaps China may be an exception. We do not know enough about it to speak, but consider what the Roman and Greek world was when Christianity appeared. It was full of superstition, not of infidelity. There was much unbelief in all as regards their mythology, and in every educated man, as to eternal punishment. But there was no casting off the idea of religion, and of unseen powers who governed the world. When they spoke of Fate, even here they considered that there was a great moral governance of the world carried on by fated laws. Their first principles were the same as ours. Even among the sceptics of Athens, St. Paul could appeal to the Unknown God. Even to the ignorant populace of Lystra he could speak of the living God who did them good from heaven. And so when the northern barbarians came down at a later age, they, amid all their superstitions, were believers in an unseen Providence and in the moral law. But we are now coming to a time when the world does not acknowledge our first principles. Of course I do not deny that, as in the revolted kingdom of Israel, there will be a remnant. The history of Elias is here a great consolation for us, for he was told from heaven that even in that time of idolatrous apostasy, there were seven thousand men who had not bowed their knees to Baal. Much more it may be expected now, when our Lord has come and the Gospel been preached to the whole world, that there will be a remnant who belong to the soul of the Church, though their eyes are not opened to acknowledge her who is their true Mother. But I speak first of the educated world, scientific, literary, political, professional, artistic—and next of the mass of town population, the two great classes on which the fortunes of England are turning: the thinking, speaking and acting England. My Brethren, you are coming into a world, if present appearances do not deceive, such as priests never came into before, that is, so far forth as you do go into it, so far as you go beyond your flocks, and so far as those flocks may be in great danger as under the influence of the prevailing epidemic.

That the discipline of a seminary is just that which is suited to meet the present state of things, it does not become me to attempt to suggest to you now—you, who have so much better, and so much more authoritative advisers—but I may be allowed perhaps to follow up what I have said to such conclusions as it seems to point to.

1. A seminary is the only true guarantee for the creation of the ecclesiastical spirit. And this is the primary and true weapon for meeting the age, not controversy. Of course every Catholic should have an intelligent appreciation of his religion, as St. Peter says, but still controversy is not the instrument by which the world is to be resisted and overcome. And this we shall see if we study that epistle, which comes with an authority of its own, as being put by the Holy Spirit into the mouth of him who was the chief of the Apostles. What he addresses to all Christians, is especially suitable for priests. Indeed he wrote it at a time when the duties of one and the other, as against the heathen world, were the same. In the first place he reminds them of what they really *were* as Christians, and surely we should take these words as belonging especially to us ecclesiastics. "You are a chosen generation, a kingly priesthood, a holy nation, a purchased people ..." (1 Pet 2:9).

In this ecclesiastical spirit, I will but mention a spirit of seriousness or recollection. We must gain the habit of feeling that we are in God's presence, that He sees what we are doing; and a liking that He does so, a love of knowing it, a delight in the reflection, "Thou, God, seest me." A priest who feels this deeply will never misbehave himself in mixed society. It will keep him from over-familiarity with any of his people; it will keep him from too many words, from imprudent or unwise speaking; it will teach him to rule his thoughts. It will be a principle of detachment between him and even his own people; for he who is accustomed to lean on the Unseen God, will never be able really to attach himself to any of His creatures. And thus an elevation of mind will be created, which is the true weapon which he must use against the infidelity of the world. (Hence, what St. Peter says: 1 Pet 2:12, 15; 3:16.)

Now this I consider to be the true weapon by which the infidelity of the world is to be met.

2. And next, most important in the same warfare, and here too you will see how it is connected with a Seminary, is a sound, accurate, complete knowledge of Catholic theology. This, though it is not controversial, is the best weapon (after a good life) *in* controversy. Any child, well instructed in the catechism, is, without intending it, a real missioner. And why? Because the world is full of doubtings and uncertainty, and of inconsistent doctrine—a clear consistent idea of revealed truth, on the contrary, cannot be found outside of the Catholic Church. Consistency, completeness, is a persuasive argument for a system being true. Certainly if it be inconsistent, it is not truth.